A DREAM
Surpassing Every Impasse

HANS HERLINGER
with LAUREL MARSHFIELD

A DREAM
Surpassing Every Impasse

Becoming a Doctor Against All Odds:
As an Austrian Jew,
On the Eve of World War II
A MEMOIR

To order additional copies of this book, contact:
Xlibris Corporation
1-888-795-4274
www.Xlibris.com
Orders@Xlibris.com
31544

This book

is dedicated

with all my love

to my parents

Ernst Herlinger

Else Friedrich Herlinger

CONTENTS

Where there was tempest and darkness
There shall be stillness and light
        And the turbulent waters
Turn to a path at your feet.

Kurt Weill
Der Silbersee, Ein Wintermächen

ACKNOWLEDGMENTS

My heartfelt gratitude goes to my dear friend, Betty Schmidt, who not only encouraged me to write this memoir, she stayed with me as I did so, every single step of the way. Her dedication to this book is behind every page.

My equally heartfelt thanks go to my sons, John Herlinger and Charles Herlinger. Their many contributions to this memoir, like the constancy of their support, have been touching and most welcome.

I also wish to acknowledge all of my friends—those who appear in these pages, and those who do not. Thank you for your company and the warmth of your smiles: my life has been endlessly enriched by your friendship.

And to my collaborator and writer, Laurel Marshfield, I owe my sincerest thanks. Without her help, interest, and understanding, I simply could not have completed my memoir.

Finally, I would like to acknowledge Maggie Herlinger, my canine companion in daily life. Her joyfulness is an unending inspiration to me, and her small, lively presence a continuous comfort.

FOREWORD

The Penn Years: My Professional Association and Friendship with Hans Herlinger

By Igor Laufer

Hans Herlinger's name and reputation preceded my initial London meeting with him by several years. In the early 1970s, when I was a young radiologist beginning my career in gastrointestinal radiology at McMaster University Medical Center in Ontario, Canada, I frequently heard Dr. Herlinger spoken of in glowing terms. My department chief, Dr. W. Peter Cockshott, described Herlinger's consummate skills in many aspects of radiology, including ultrasound and mammography. But particular praise went to his work in gastrointestinal radiology, especially the barium studies and angiography. Herlinger was then quite well known in European medical circles, and Dr. Cockshott had trained in Edinburgh where he became well acquainted with Herlinger's reputation in Europe.

Then an opportunity arose that would prove fateful for both Dr. Herlinger and myself. In 1975, when he had been Chairman of Radiology at St. James's University Hospital in Leeds, England for nearly a decade, I was invited to participate in a symposium at London's St. Georges Hospital. Scanning the program for this event, I immediately noticed that the famous Dr. Herlinger was also a speaker on the program. It seemed the perfect time to visit him in Leeds and observe his work, as he was one of the first in England and, for that matter, all of Europe, to undertake double contrast gastrointestinal studies.

Though I was half Dr. Herlinger's age, he generously shared his work with me, as I was engaged in performing the same type of GI studies in

Canada. I felt privileged to watch him complete several angiographies, as well as his variation on the double contrast technique for viewing the stomach. This particular methodology made far more detailed radiological pictures possible. And these pictures, in turn, allowed the discovery of much smaller abnormalities (gastric cancers, tumors, and ulcers) that were at an earlier stage of their development. Most simply, this was because the stomach would be radiologically photographed two times: first, barium material made the outline of the organ visible; second, gas was used to blow up or distend it, making the interior visible. The resulting images were a thing of great beauty to radiologists. But, in layperson terms, the difference between this new double contrast technique, using barium and a distending agent, versus the older single contrast technique, using barium alone, was the equivalent of looking at a patient's body with the clothes off, and the clothes on. The former obviously resulted in much better medical treatment.

During our initial meeting in the mid-1970s, Dr. Herlinger and I talked about all manner of things in addition to medicine, but I remember particularly well our drive from Leeds to London. It was then he told me something that would later alter both our lives, and those of many others, as well. The National Health Service in England had imposed a mandatory retirement age for all medical professionals, which meant that he would face retirement at age sixty-five. This was then a prospect just five years away, he told me, and one he did not at all welcome because his work was of central importance to him. What was obvious to me, however, was that his chronological age meant absolutely nothing: Herlinger was still so extraordinarily vital a man, and one quite capable of pursuing his profession for many years to come.

Fortunately, fate—or perhaps a chance combination of circumstances— intervened. The following year, in 1976, I was recruited to start and head a section of gastrointestinal radiology by Dr. Stanley Baum, the chairman of the Department of Radiology at the Hospital of the University of Pennsylvania, in Philadelphia. Developing a sub-specialized section would involve a great deal of work, and I knew I'd need some help. I thought of Dr. Herlinger, and it occurred to me that he might be interested in spending a year as a visiting professor at Penn. I called him, and he was delighted to come to the States. During the course of his first year at Penn, Dr. Herlinger proved to be a great hit, because of his expertise in all aspects of gastroenterology and radiology. Though once the year ended, he of course had to return to England. But because as I was aware of his imminent forced retirement, I proposed that he return to Penn as permanent member of our staff. This Dr. Herlinger did in 1978, and for the next twenty-five years he enjoyed a marvelous second career in the United States, becoming the acknowledged international master of radiology of the small bowel.

Shortly after Herlinger returned to Penn, he moved his primary area of investigation from gastric radiology to the small bowel work for which he would become world famous. Prior to Herlinger's refinement of the double contrast method for use with the small bowel, the results of small bowel radiology were not particularly good. The standard radiological examination of this organ involves barium, which the patient swallows, and which the radiologist hopes will pass through to the small bowel in a few hours. With the double contrast method, or enteroclysis, a tube is passed through the patient's nose and manipulated into the small bowel. Once in place, the bowel is infused with barium directly, followed by methylcellulose to distend it, thus causing it to be translucent and visible with radiography. This dramatically improves the ability to detect adhesions (obstructive scar tissue that is usually a result of surgery), as well as tumors, arteriovenous malformations, Crohn's disease, and Celiac disease. Quite simply, this provides a far more elegant examination of the small bowel.

But Dr. Herlinger was additionally well-known for performing the very meticulous work of making sure that all the conditions for radiologic images were correct, that they were produced of the right area, and that the exposures were perfect. His work was so good, in fact, that he brought a definite notoriety to Penn because of it. Radiologists from other academic medical centers around the country came to HUP in order to learn enterocylsis by watching him at work. At the same time, physicians along the East Coast who wanted to refer their patients to the best in the field always sent them to Dr. Herlinger. In other words, he was "it" in this area of specialization. Fittingly, there is an historical timeline on our departmental website with a single entry for 1978 that reads: "Hans Herlinger developed the technique of methylcellulose double contrast small bowel study (Enteroclysis)."

But there were many other ways that Dr. Herlinger contributed to the excellence of our department. His presence on our faculty helped strengthen our ties with British and European radiology. Most notably, there were the international courses he organized, among them "Gastroenterology for Radiologists" which integrated the clinical aspects of GI radiology with GI medicine for enhanced understanding, and which took place in Leeds, England. Members of our faculty were regular participants, and they benefited greatly by interacting with their European colleagues. Then, in 1981 and 1982, he organized courses in collaboration with faculty at the University of Vienna that were held at the Hofburg Palace. Attending these, we found ourselves treated like royalty. They were simply magnificent professional and social occasions for everyone. All this had never happened before. The international reach of our department was greatly strengthened—a tendency I myself applauded and supported, having immigrated from Czechoslovakia to Canada, and later on, to the United States.

But Dr. Herlinger's skill with languages, his ability to present papers in German, Italian, and French (and the fact that the Europeans viewed him as one of their own who had "made good" in America), made him very popular internationally. He was invited to lecture all over the world, for years. But perhaps the most touching aspect of his highly effective work in fostering medical international relations was the fact that, in 1979, he was awarded an honorary doctor of medicine degree from the University of Graz. This was the same medical school that Herlinger would have graduated from in the 1930s, had the Nazi rise to power not forced him to flee Austria before taking the final exams for his degree. At last, a great wrong seemed partially righted. The major newspapers in Graz featured the story of Herlinger's honorary medical degree—as if to underscore the Austrian effort to rectify the past. Hans himself spoke of it often, something he never did with any of his other honors and awards. It obviously meant a great deal to him.

During his decades at Penn, Dr. Herlinger pursued his work with vigor and dedication, always arriving at his office promptly at 7:00 in the morning. When he was still going strong at seventy-four years of age, we wanted to show our appreciation by throwing a "non-retirement" surprise party. In order to keep the real reason for this event a secret, we printed invitations to the "Bar Mitzvah" of the GI radiology section (that year was the department's thirteenth). Herlinger's invitation was printed with a cocktail hour that was thirty minutes later. And so, when he arrived, there were fifty people—faculty, technologists, students—already waiting at Penn's Wharton Sinkler estate. His surprise was evident, but he graciously rose to the occasion as our honoree.

We presented him with a leatherbound copy of his most recent book, *Clinical Radiology of the Small Intestine*, one of two Herlinger books that are considered the classic and definitive texts on small bowel imaging. And we gave him a photo album of his years at Penn: pictures of his work in the department, and of colleagues, radiographers, and department secretaries, as well as photos of the annual pool party he hosted each summer at his house in Penn Valley. All of us still remember that evening in 1989 as an important departmental occasion.

Throughout his career, Herlinger received innumerable awards, but by far the most prestigious was the Cannon Medal, the highest honor there is in our field. The Cannon Medal was awarded for lifetime achievement in GI radiology, and presented to Dr. Herlinger in Bermuda in 1996. Before the formal ceremony, a large group of Herlinger's former trainees at Penn, both residents and fellows, who had gathered on the island for the occasion, threw a dinner party in his honor. They wanted to acknowledge this significant public recognition of his life's work.

Though this was an undeniably special occasion, there was a lively tradition of throwing semi-formal as well as formal parties in Penn's GI radiology department. And whenever we had a sit-down dinner or some other formal occasion, Hans would act as our sommelier. Expertly, he would study the wine list, make excellent choices, and rise to start off the toasts. Our general feeling was that he added a much-needed touch of cosmopolitan class to a group of "scruffy" (by comparison) young Americans. And, of course, everybody loved him. Even now, when I travel to places around the world for medical conferences, everyone always eagerly inquires, "How's Hans?"

Hans Herlinger leaves a legacy of excellence and innovation on both sides of the Atlantic and, indeed, throughout the world. But for me, and for our department at Penn, it was a stroke of incredible good luck that our need for his assistance coincided with his impending retirement from St. James' Hospital in Leeds.

The second career he cultivated, during what would be considered—purely from a chronological perspective—his post-retirement years, held within its twenty-five year span his most important work, and his major contribution to medicine. Hans has lived many lives during his long and fruitful life. But we feel quite fortunate, indeed, that this great yet very modest man came to the United States, and lived a few of his lives with us.

PREFACE

Hans Herlinger:
Teacher, Mentor, Colleague, Friend

By Marc Levine

When I was a junior resident in the late 1970s at the Hospital of the University of Pennsylvania, my first encounters with Dr. Herlinger were a little intimidating. Mostly, I was struck by his daunting appearance and manner. The regal eyebrows, the impeccable attire, and the distinguished voice all seemed more appropriate for a British barrister than a gastrointestinal radiologist. He even had a way of making the intestines sound aristocratically austere: the small bowel's terminal section became, in his pronunciation, the "eye-leum," not the more pedestrian-sounding "ileum" that I'd heard so many times before. As if all that were not enough to frighten a radiology neophyte like myself, Herlinger also bore an uncanny resemblance to the actor Gregory Peck—especially Peck in his role as Atticus Finch in "To Kill a Mockingbird." Like Peck, Hans had a commanding presence that drew both attention and respect. During my first GI rotation, when I finally worked up the nerve to tell him how much he looked like the famous actor, Dr. Herlinger answered with his trademark wry humor.

"No, my boy," he quipped. "It is Gregory Peck who looks like me!"

Of course, I could not help but notice the twinkle in Herlinger's eyes. I liked the lack of self-importance his humorous response implied, and from then on I was determined to learn as much as possible from this exceedingly charming man.

When I became better acquainted with Dr. Herlinger, I realized that he was not just charming and aristocratic, albeit unself-consciously so.

19

He was a brilliant and dedicated radiologist with tremendous passion for gastrointestinal radiology. As Herlinger became known as a world-class expert in all aspects of small bowel radiology, I watched him become frustrated by existing radiologic techniques for examining the small intestine. I was then privileged to witness his remarkable development of enteroclysis, an exquisite new technique for examining the small intestine. Using enteroclysis, previously hidden lesions in the small intestine appeared as if lit by a brilliant halogen light—rather than as if illuminated by flickering candlelight. Dr. Herlinger's role in its development was forever commemorated by the name of the special barium solution the procedure uses. It is called "Entero-H"—with the "H," of course, standing for Herlinger.

During his twenty-five years at Penn, Dr. Herlinger explored virtually every aspect of small bowel disease, describing in a series of seminal papers a host of pathologic conditions involving the small intestine and their radiologic appearances. Ultimately, he chronicled his numerous observations and findings in a magnificent treatise, *Clinical Radiology of the Small Intestine*, published by W. B. Saunders in 1989, with a second edition published by Springer-Verlag in 1999. These encyclopedic and classic works have long assumed a prominent place on the library shelves of gastrointestinal radiologists around the world.

Along with his singular accomplishments as a diagnostic innovator and researcher, Hans also excelled at teaching and interacting with residents and fellows on Penn's GI radiology service. He always led the liveliest sessions when reviewing the day's cases with his trainees, though perhaps his greatest joy came from presenting his expert knowledge on a broader stage. Whether Hans was giving an honorary lecture to hundreds of leading European radiologists at an international radiology meeting in Vienna, or giving a morning conference for radiology residents, he was always an eloquent speaker. Whatever the subject matter, his lectures were invariably clear and cogent, distilling even the most complex material into its most important essential elements. As a result, his presentations were uniformly anticipated and savored by trainees and experienced radiologists alike.

Quite simply, it must be said that Dr. Herlinger was a spectacular gastrointestinal radiologist, one whose teaching, research, clinical skills and accomplishments established him as a leader in his field. All this would surely distinguish a radiologist so gifted at the peak of his career, but what makes Herlinger so remarkable is that he performed these feats at an age when most physicians would be enjoying their retirement years. Herlinger's major accomplishments and contributions were all made during the sixth, seventh, and eighth decades of his life, when he had the energy, ambition, and stamina to reinvent and revitalize small bowel radiology and, at the same time, his own career.

As for my own career, some years after I became one of Dr. Herlinger's trainees, I finished my residency and joined the GI radiology faculty at Penn. Hans then became not only my mentor, but my colleague and friend. Having known him in all these capacities, I can say that Hans Herlinger is one of the few truly extraordinary people in our field whom I've been privileged to know.

Besides, he is someone Gregory Peck was fortunate enough to look like.

PROLOGUE

My Friend, Hans Herlinger

By Susan Giesecke Bloom

Our friendship began in the mid-1970s when Hans Herlinger, the famous visiting professor from Leeds, England, joined the Hospital of the University of Pennsylvania Radiology Department where I was a resident. Talkative and outgoing, I sought out the new professor and engaged him in conversations that led to our thirty-year friendship. Quite soon after our initial meeting, our talk continued over dinner in my home, where I traded home-cooked meals for valuable radiology pointers and wonderful insights into Hans' life.

Years later, after my husband and I moved to Reading, about an hour northwest of Philadelphia, I occasionally stopped for an early dinner at Hans' house on my way out of the city. He always set a proper table in the den, arranging on its linen tablecloth the meal he picked up from a local gourmet shop. The perfect host, Hans often had a new Aquavit or other exotic drink for me to try, and we spent the next few hours talking and eating, before home drew me away. Sometimes, our conversation focused on radiology, or a problem I was having in my department, but often it centered on Hans' experiences as a young man. His early life in Europe and his life during the war years were especially fascinating. I felt privileged to share his confidence, touched that he would discuss this part of his life with me.

Some years later, when Hans was awarded the Cannon Medal, and his colleagues, family, and friends flew to Bermuda for the occasion, I remember talking with his sons at the departmental party held before the presentation ceremony. The subject of conversation soon turned to their father's life as a young man, and I was surprised that John and Charles did not know more about its details. Later on, Hans revealed that he, like many survivors, told his sons relatively little, preferring not to weigh them down with his painful past.

This reticence with his sons did not, however, stop Hans from driving to Washington, D.C. with me to visit the United States Holocaust Memorial Museum, a year or so after it first opened. The banter between us as we drove to D.C. flowed easily, but once we arrived and became immersed in the museum's exhibits, we barely spoke at all. Walking through that dramatically recreated history of the 1930s, Hans reached for my hand and gripped it tightly. Several times, as we made our way through all the exhibits, he became choked-up with emotion. When we finally came to the endless names of victims displayed on the museum's walls, he scanned them avidly—looking for family, friends, his former fiancée—but to no avail. The names he sought simply were not there. We returned to Philadelphia in uncharacteristic silence. What we'd just seen made all conversation seem trivial by comparison, and so talk was impossible.

More characteristically, though, our times together centered on food as well as talk. For many years, Hans joined our family table in celebration of the Jewish holidays, seeming to connect with his Jewish roots in this way.

Occasionally, he brought along his beloved miniature dachshund, Jackie, to share in the festivities—much to the delight of our grandchildren.

For my birthday in 1992, my husband gave me two weeks of gourmet cooking lessons at a famous Philadelphia restaurant, and that necessitated a stay in the city at the Bellevue Hotel. Knowing how much I love champagne, Hans insisted on treating me to two of the finest bottles the hotel had to offer, with a birthday dinner. I can't remember what we ate that evening, but I will never forget what we drank.

On many other occasions, a professional conference provided an opportunity for us to break bread together, and we often met for dinner while attending radiology meetings in Chicago. After I chose the restaurant and Hans picked the wine, we'd share a lot of laughs over pasta and a good bottle of claret in the windy city.

Hans, my husband, and I also enjoyed curry and gin together in London; margaritas, salsa and chips on the balcony of our Florida home; and turkey at our Thanksgiving table. Each time of shared conviviality was an opportunity to recount the stories of our lives and deepen our friendship.

The medical community knows Hans as a dedicated scholar and clinician. I am triply blessed to know him as a mentor, a colleague, and most importantly, as a dear, warm and caring friend.

Looking out to sea and contemplating my uncertain future,
soon after my forced exile from Austria in 1938.

INTRODUCTION

Looking Back:
Why I Wrote This Memoir

W hen I was a boy in Graz, Austria, and my parents, grandparents, uncles, and aunts seemed a fixed firmament of adults shining down like stars upon my young life, I could not have imagined the story my memoir tells.

Because I could not have imagined World War II, the war that later became so entwined with my own personal history that it was the defining event of my life. For when I was a naïve and inexperienced medical student of twenty-three, the war forced me to leave forever the happy and secure world I'd always known, to dive headfirst in a sea of uncertainty, loss, and fear. The perpetrators of this war destroyed my home and family, murdered my father, my relatives, and my fiancée, and forced those few of us who survived to disperse over several continents.

Aside from my life and two suitcases of belongings, the only other possession that survived the war was my dream of becoming a doctor. Looking back, I realize how valuable and essential a possession that was.

As a life-defining vision of my future, it helped me to "surpass every impasse." Without it, I cannot know how I might have fared. For it was in pursuit of this dream that I made my way to the temporary safety of Malta—there to enroll in the school of medicine at the Royal University in Valletta. Later on, while being held for years in British internment camps in Palestine and Entebbe, Uganda, I found useful and engaging work as a partially trained physician. Medicine saved my sanity by occupying my mind, just as pursuing the dream of my future profession took me, time and again, out of harm's way.

But there was another dynamic involved. While the extreme circumstances the war created led me to call upon a degree of resourcefulness and persistence I didn't yet know I possessed, my efforts were always matched by fortuitous circumstances totally outside my control. Each time it looked as if I couldn't possibly continue, a path appeared out of thin air. But if I had not held so tightly to my dream of a career in medicine, I cannot be certain a path would have appeared. If my story serves to illustrate any particular life principle at all, it would seem to be this one: our deepest and most cherished dreams may, quite literally, save our lives. They do so in a number of ways. Not only do our dreams prove life-defining, thus protecting us from uncertainty of a most distressing and chaotic sort. They offer a lifelong pursuit, as well, the lack of which deprives us of both ballast and rudder, while we sail the seas of constant change, throughout our lives. Further, our dreams may lead us to encounter our best selves. In my own case, there came a point when it seemed I might have been spared during the war because there was something I was meant to do. Though as my story reveals, it was not until I entered my sixth decade that this "something" finally became clear.

There is one other idea I should like to touch on here, by way of an introduction to my memoir. When I later married and became the father of two sons, I found myself unwilling to disturb their childhood innocence with stories about the war. I did not want that horror to invade their lives as it had mine. And so I remained relatively silent about my early life, thinking I might protect them in this way from what our family suffered. Eventually, I did tell them some stories about the Austrian and Yugoslav Herlingers, and our Hungarian relatives on my mother's side, the Friedrichs (my wife, Betty Nield Herlinger, was thoroughly English). But this book is an effort to finally tell my story completely, from beginning to end. For as generations multiply, and sons and daughters are born, it is my hope that it will serve as a written legacy, one filling the historical gaps, despite all that was lost to our family—one of many millions torn apart during that terrible war.

I cannot avoid this final realization, too. Those of us who somehow escaped death during World War II should perhaps attempt to bear witness, not only to our own lives as shaped by the war, but to the lives of those who were silenced by it. And so I have tried to remember a few of those people, both relatives and friends, who touched my life before and during the war years, and who thus became a part of how I affected others, in turn.

In this, and other ways, as well, I believe that those who died live on.

CHAPTER ONE

Trieste, Italy
Fall ~ 1938

I n the fall of 1938, the blue Adriatic Sea was as calm as my childhood memory of it, a memory formed on family holidays in Abbazia, a resort near Venice—though I myself was far from calm. As I studied the sea's sleepily hypnotic waves, while sipping espresso at an outdoor café in the seaport town of Trieste, a hundred or so kilometers east of Abbazia, I was surrounded by obstacles.

My life was, in fact, at an impasse. But as a young man of twenty-three, I did not of course know how my future might unfold. And so, I did not realize that this was merely the first in a series of impasses, all poised to appear in my life, one after another—as if mailed from that invisible place known as fate. As I watched the waves rise and fall, disappearing instantly into the ceaselessly moving sea, I knew nothing of my fate. All I knew was that the rich, slightly acrid taste of the coffee, and the company of four fellow Austrians—who were forced as I was into exile—did nothing to dispel the frustration and despair I then felt, the numb disbelief. What transpired, recently, was fantastical and altogether unreal.

Only a week ago, I kissed my mother, Elserl, goodbye, and said my farewells to Father and my younger brother, Pauli. Hoping to spare us all too many painful feelings, I somewhat shortened my leavetaking before boarding a small propeller plane for Venice, on the Adriatic coast of Italy. My decision to leave Austria was not a real one; there was simply no other choice within reason. Either go into voluntary exile, I was advised by the police, or be re-arrested and imprisoned once again.

In the early spring and summer, I was held with a group of about thirty others in a makeshift prison, all of us arrested as members of the so-called Jewish leadership. With the infiltration of Nazi policies and agendas into Austrian politics, any affiliation with Jewish activities was suspect; now, apparently, it was considered an outright crime. But since my leadership role was neither politically significant nor important in any real way, it seemed a bogus and empty charge.

Throughout my mid-teens and early twenties, I was a member of three Jewish organizations for young people. The most recent of these was a social service group that I eventually chaired. We welcomed and supported Jewish students from Eastern Europe, when they came to study at my university in Graz. Earlier on, I was a member of Charitas, a college fraternity, and earlier still, I was involved in the youth division of Betar, a Zionist organization with a quasi-military flavor. My brother Pauli and I joined Betar in 1933, soon after Hitler's troubling ascension as chancellor of Germany.

But Betar for youth was hardly a military force to be reckoned with. Mainly a display of regimentation, the group dispensed blue and white uniforms to boys and girls between the ages of twelve and sixteen, and conducted a two-week training camp in Carynthia, a western province of Austria. This camp offered instruction in proper marching techniques, interspersed with Zionist lectures about a Jewish homeland, located in a somewhat mythical Palestine. After graduating from Betar training as an officer, or *Samal Aleph Aleph* in Hebrew (one of the few terms I can still recall in that language, though as an adult I was fluent in five languages), I found myself marching, at age sixteen, through Graz's untrafficked warehouse district, at the head of a column of girls. My "troops" wore the feminine rank-and-file uniform of blue skirts with white blouses, while I myself wore the more military attire of an officer: blue trousers, a white shirt, a broad leather belt with shoulder strap, and a brimmed cap. Other of our official activities included walking tours through the alpine foothills surrounding Graz, and occasional inspections by the Viennese commandant for all the Betarist groups in Austria. But the goals of the Betar movement were not, finally, mine. My participation was part of an evolving search that began in my teens—for that purpose in life I might embrace as my own.

Two years later, upon entering the university, I continued this search through my induction into the fraternal Jewish organization known as Charitas, or Charity. Modeled after German student groups, Charitas inculcated the manly virtues of strength and courage by engaging its members in tireless saber dueling practice. When not wielding our swords, we took up another athletic pursuit: drinking keg after keg of good Austrian beer while loudly singing student songs. "Oh, let us enjoy ourselves while we are still young," we sang heartily (though not in German but, with added effect, in Latin), "for after our jolly youth," we knowingly observed (while still safely ensconced within our *own* youth), ". . . after our jolly youth, comes the sad state of age."

It was easier to sing such songs in boisterous unison while downing stein after frothy stein. Songs like this one also served as easy justification for our competitive bouts of beer-drinking, a practice which later seemed as pointless and foolhardy to me as our vigorous sparing with sabers. Though I must admit that, after more than one all-too-drunken occasion, I required the assistance of my saber partners to stumble, with great difficulty, home. But this is how I learned that the ill-fitting name of "Charity" possessed a hidden relevance.

Despite these youthful rites of passage, as I now see that they were (although, at the time, they appeared far more significant; I felt somewhat as if I were facing induction into adulthood), this period did result in one life-defining decision. My father wanted me to study law, believing I was most useful to the family grain importing business as an attorney. I wanted to please my father, and so dutifully took introductory classes in various aspects of the law. But nothing about legal principles and distinctions moved me in the slightest. Medicine, on the other hand, appealed from the start. I was unable to stay away, and attended medical lectures as often as possible during a semester of tedious legal study. When I finally told Father that law did not command even a small part of my interest, in the way medicine so completely did, he gradually accepted the inevitable. His eldest son was not going to join him in the family business, but would study medicine, instead, and become a doctor.

During my five years at Karl Frazen's University in Graz, I passed exams for the first "Rigorosum" in my second year, continuing through rotations in internal medicine and surgery during the remaining three and a half years of my core medical training. My overarching plan was simple and straightforward: to sit for my final exams, get my degree, and marry my fiancée, Lizzie Biró. Lizzie and I were childhood playmates, as she was the daughter of family friends. Over the course of time, our friendship blossomed into romance, and now we were eager to marry, begin our life together, and start a family.

But as I was nearing completion with my medical studies, and preparing for my final exams, I was unable to ignore the political darkness enveloping the world beyond my university in Graz. Germany, led by Hitler, was then waging a campaign that clearly revealed the extreme anti-Semitism at the heart of the Nazi agenda. German Jews were under attack, and with the passage of the "Nuremberg Race Laws" in 1935, were denied even the most basic civil rights. The Jewish population living in Graz was relatively small. Most Austrian Jews lived in Vienna, though the country as a whole possessed fewer than 200,000 Jewish residents. In fact, during the entire twelve years of my schooling before entering the university, I was the only boy with a Jewish background. And, as I must admit, I was not overly aware of my religious heritage. For one thing, I hadn't experienced that most intimate of Jewish rituals, the *Bris*, or circumcision, always performed on eight-day-old baby boys by a rabbi. For another, I was so uninspired during the only instruction in Judaism I ever received, that I avoided these classes as much as possible. As a result, the Rabbi of Graz, who taught them, gave me low grades. This made me think of him in a negative light, since I was a good student used to getting good grades. His frequent complaints to my parents about my poor class attendance did not endear him to me, either. And yet, it was the Rabbi of Graz who gave me a very prescient gift.

On the occasion of a small party to celebrate my thirteenth birthday, which I was given in lieu of the more traditional *Bar Mitzvah* my younger brother later celebrated, he presented me with a book about an adventurer in Africa. This was a country that later figured importantly in my training as a medical doctor, so perhaps this rabbi was wiser than I gave him credit for being.

Despite it all, I *was* Jewish, though it certainly never occurred to me this represented any particular liability. I felt everyone had the right to be who they were—including, of course, me. But against this benign backdrop, there came a time when catastrophic political events, all of them orchestrated to the tune of Nazi fanaticism, forced their way into the studious daily routine of my life.

It was early morning, during the first week of February, a little over one month before the *Anschluss*, the annexation of Austria by Germany's "Third Reich," solidifying German rule in my country. On that morning, the knocking at our front door sounded both officious and urgent. Father went to answer, and two Austrian policemen entered. They announced that I, the Herlinger's eldest son, was under arrest. There was a brief discussion. I was allowed to gather a few articles of clothing and some books. Then off I walked through the streets of Graz with these middle-aged Austrians on either side of me, as if attending a family funeral in another part of town. We walked and walked. Forty-five minutes of walking later, we arrived at the top of a hill—traversing cobble-stoned streets, once we entered the older section of Graz—and they escorted me to a building standing in a group of buildings arranged around a square. This was the central police station. I was taken into a large common room, slightly below courtyard level. Those arrested with me included thirty or so men of varying ages, all considered in some way active in Jewish affairs. It did not cheer me to notice that the bearded and portly Rabbi of Graz was among those men sitting at a long wooden table in the room's center. Here we remained, herded together for more than two months. Each day began by stacking the mattresses we slept on during the night in a far corner. Outdoor exercise followed, calisthenics and running conducted by a good-natured local policeman. Some, including the overweight Rabbi, were exempt from these exertions for medical reasons. The rest of our time was spent reading or playing cards, and talking among ourselves.

Thankfully, I did not feel totally cut off from the innocent goodness of family life. My mother was able to visit often (she was on friendly terms with one of our guards), and enlivened my prison diet with delicious ham or cheese sandwiches and pastries made comfortingly at home. But we were not allowed to see each other. Her brief messages ("All is well. We are well, and hope you will soon be out of prison."), were conveyed by the same guard who slipped me her carefully wrapped packages of food.

Among those arrested with me was Dr. Otto Loewi, a Nobel Prize winner whose lectures I attended at the University in Graz. His discovery—the specific chemicals the human body uses to transmit nerve impulses through the sympathetic nervous system—earned him the 1936 laureate in Physiology or Medicine. Since Dr. Loewi's older son, also named Otto, was a student in my class at medical school, I was acquainted with the senior Otto in a more personal way, having socialized with his family in their home.

Dr. Loewi kindly spent hours discussing various ways of constructing a medical future for myself outside Austria. Because of my familiarity with Italy, he told me where to inquire about continuing my education in that country. And he mentioned opportunities in the United States, something about which I was then totally ignorant. (A few years after Dr. Loewi's imprisonment in Graz, he was allowed to immigrate to the United

States—though not before he was forced to deposit his Nobel laureate prize money in a bank account that the Nazis immediately pilfered.)

But the situation soon worsened for many of us, as our good-natured Austrian guard was replaced by a stern SA man, a Nazi German stormtrooper who delighted in making the morning exercises difficult for those who were unable to keep up. He obviously hoped the more strenuous regimen was physically punishing. In my case, this daily demand for greater exertion simply made me even more fit than before. And since I'd always been a very fast runner, I secretly delighted in outrunning everyone else, a feat which seemed a minor triumph over my imprisonment. Though of course I concealed my satisfaction, knowing I should keep this covert method of psychological survival to myself.

All of us were mainly preoccupied with the unanswerable question of when we might regain our freedom. And so, were either immersed in our own turbulent thoughts, or else trying to escape the claustrophobia of our confinement by losing ourselves in the mental freedom offered by books. I'd always loved to read, and often did so until late at night (and was admonished by my father the next day, as he thought I needed the sleep to do well in school). Books readily became a comfort to me in those drab and frustrating circumstances. Chief among the volumes I brought with me to jail were a few medical texts that I studied daily, intent upon preparing for my final exams.

Toward the end of our incarceration, we were removed from the common room and placed in locked cells, with three of us to a cell. My brother, Pauli, who was arrested a month or so after I was, initially shared a cell with me. When we had a disagreement (both of us were struggling, I realized much later, to take on the more defined identity of early adulthood), he requested relocation to another cell.

Then, one morning, we heard an uncharacteristically noisy commotion. It was impossible, at first, to know what was happening, since the end of the hallway was only partly visible from the small window centered in our cell door. Shouts and curses were interspersed with the sound of stumbling feet. Later on, we learned that when the Nazis took over our local government, they imprisoned the Christian Socialist Party politicians then in office, replacing them with officials more sympathetic to Nazi political and social aims. These local politicians were now being carted off to Dachau where they probably perished. It was the first time any of us heard that horrible, haunting name for one of Hitler's death camps, and it was a name that later meant a great deal more to me, than it did just then.

Some weeks later, there was a completely unexpected turn of events. Quite abruptly, our captors told Pauli and me that if we signed papers agreeing to go into voluntary exile from Austria, we might regain our freedom. While this was better than remaining behind locked doors, the conditions of our release held their own form of hardship. They interrupted my medical training, just as I was about to take the exams qualifying for my degree, and meant leaving behind everything I'd ever known—my family and friends, my country. In truth, however, I was disgusted by the open-armed welcome many Austrians gave the Nazis. I adamantly declared to myself that I'd *never* return to this country I now felt utterly betrayed by.

The future was now exceedingly unsure. Not just for me, but for my whole family. We were certain of one thing, only: it was time to flee Austria. My parents applied for citizenship in Yugoslavia, as Father was born in that country, but I was making arrangements to leave sooner. My mother phoned a distant relative in Venice, and when she agreed to let me stay at her small hotel, I prepared to travel, in compliance with the terms of my release as a political prisoner, to Italy. Pauli was scheduled to arrive in Venice within a few weeks, following me into exile.

*   *   *

The flight to Venice was my first experience of airplane travel, and as my small plane rose above the earth, I felt something I'd never before felt. When the solid ground fell away beneath me, the wings of the plane took over and held me, miraculously, aloft. In those brief minutes of takeoff, flying seemed at once exhilarating and terrifying. But I was too filled with uncertainty, and the dissociated feeling that comes from a state of shock, to fully focus my attention. As nine other passengers and I flew in a southwesterly direction toward Italy, our propeller airplane barely grazed the alpine foothills bordering southern Austria, before skimming the flat countryside leading into northern Italy. Though I saw all this from a round side window, I did not take it in. There was simply no emotional room within my bruised psyche to accommodate this novel aerial view, the patchwork quilt of land so far below.

A hazy period of time later, after our small plane arrived at the airport outside Venice, I boarded a water taxi for the next leg of my journey. The small rocking waves beneath this boat were somewhat calming to me, but when we tied-up at a dock in the center of town, I disembarked awkwardly, carrying two heavy leather suitcases filled with most of my clothes and all of my medical books.

Weighed down by these bags, I began to search for the Hotel d'Aria, my aunt's hotel. Only after asking several strangers for directions (using the Italian that I loved for its musicality when I first heard it on our family vacations in Abbazia, and that I'd quickly taught myself the rudiments of after leaving the Graz prison), did I at last find the hotel's front door and ring its bell. Waiting for someone to appear, I vaguely imagined my aunt being glad to see a member of her family, albeit one from Austria. A stocky, middle-aged woman opened the door, and soon made it quite clear that I was nothing more than an imposition. Showing me to a small garret room, a room my suitcases nearly filled, she brusquely explained that her hotel was full to capacity, and this was the only room she had to offer. "Our busy season," she called out, as if in grudging apology, while descending the stairs and leaving me to my painful thoughts. This did not feel like an auspicious beginning, and it naturally depressed me even further.

Lying on the lumpy mattress with its complaining bedsprings, I stared at the room's flowered wallpaper, aware that the stinging feeling in my eyes threatened real tears. But I was so emotionally removed from everything that was happening to me, I held them back with little effort. Looking up at the ceiling's numerous fine lines, little cracks that sprouted in the warm Italian summers, I tried to see straight through them into a viable future for myself.

Instead, my thoughts drifted, returning to my time in medical school. In my daydream, I saw myself sitting in the small nooks and crannies of the medical library, looking up medical references in the fading light of late afternoon. I was happy there. Recalling this past happiness, I was able to smile. Then the hospital wards appeared vividly in my memory, the rows of beds in the early hours after midnight, when I was the resident on duty. It was my considerable responsibility to decide whether a patient required an urgent surgical procedure that I was able to perform myself (inserting a tube around an obstruction, incising an abscess). Or whether a medical crisis was severe enough that a surgeon needed to take over, performing an operation later that morning. A few of these surgeons and attending physicians, who were also our professors in the medical school, I admired greatly and hoped to emulate. They won my admiration for their fine combination of experience and skill, their seemingly boundless knowledge, and their considerable patience as teachers. To me, medicine was everything worth doing, and I loved it—especially surgery.

My daydream shifted to the inguinal or incarcerated hernia operation I performed toward the end of my training, while observed by the senior surgeon who stood beside me. After dissecting the herniated section of the patient's small bowel, I removed the part that was gangrenous, about seven centimeters in length, and placed it in a bowl held by a surgical nurse. I then rejoined the two ends of bowel, stitching them together with the cat-gut thread the patient's body would gradually absorb without a trace. I finished by repairing the abdominal muscle wall, suturing together the fascia and the skin, and closing the wound with surgical clips. When these were opened after healing was complete, they would drop easily away.

I remembered how tremendously elated I felt after performing this procedure. Though it was the sort of surgery I assisted with on many occasions, this was the first time I completed the entire operation myself. More than anything else, this post-surgical feeling of exhilaration convinced me that medicine was the road my life should take.

After just a day or two at my aunt's hotel, and though my pockets contained only a few English pounds and some Italian lira, I decided to leave because I felt unwelcome. Staying was an insult I had no stomach for, especially on the heels of my forced exile from Austria. I took a bus to Lovrana, a small village several kilometers away, and phoned Pauli to tell him of this change of plans. He joined me there soon after, and we shared a room, relatively peacefully, on the top floor of an inexpensive hotel on the main street.

From Lovrana, I one day arranged to meet several acquaintances in Trieste. These were the compatriots with whom I was sitting at that outdoor café in September of 1938. As we talked, it became clear that their plans were not destroyed by political upheaval, as mine were. They were going to take this opportunity to emigrate from Austria to Palestine and establish themselves there (in what many then hoped would become a Jewish homeland). I, on the other hand, was devastated by this turn of events, having no idea how to continue my life's plan of earning my medical degree and becoming a doctor. The several alternative options I managed to assemble were not at all appealing.

One option was to join my compatriots in immigrating to Palestine, where I envisioned a life spent fighting in an army, or else digging endless ditches in a settlement. Another was to accept an offer of employment from my fiancée's father. He owned a building materials business in Hungary and had several business partners in Milan. I envisioned this job as not only uninspiring but risky: the political situation was far too unstable to imagine a secure future in either Hungary or Italy. But by far the worst part of these alternatives was that both would swallow my dream of becoming a doctor. My one remaining option did not appear viable, either: to complete my medical degree at the University of Milan was unwise, because such a degree was not recognized outside Italy. An additional deterrent was the rise of Mussolini's fascism. It meant that I could soon be as unwelcome and unsafe in Italy, as I was in my native Austria.

As my companions talked, I looked out over the peaceful yet constantly moving sea. Studying the waves, I quite illogically hoped for an answer from the blurry blue haze floating just above the horizon. A short time later, time seemed to slow down. When someone at our table laughed, I automatically turned my head to look at him, and as I did, something appeared in the corner of my vision. Looking at this object directly, I saw a sign that said "British Trade Delegation." Immediately, I sat up in my chair. Quickly formulating a plan, I told my companions I was going over to that trade delegation office. I wanted to ask about a medical school where I might finish my degree—for I was determined to find a school recognized by England and, therefore, the world. Anything less was far too risky.

Wishing me luck, my fellow Austrians watched silently as I walked across the Piazza dell'Unita d'Italia. I could feel their gaze at my back while I opened the door to the ground floor office and walked inside. As I pulled the door shut behind me, I saw a pleasant-looking young woman sitting behind a reception desk in the main area.

"Good afternoon," I said, approaching her. I introduced myself in imperfect English (a language I'd studied, but could not manage with the ease and fluency I later acquired), and asked if I might explain my present predicament.

She smiled and said, "Of course, please do."

I described my medical studies in Graz, and how they were interrupted because of political upheaval, just as I was about to sit for my final exams. I then asked if she knew where I might complete my degree—where I might find a school recognized by England.

"Nothing comes to mind," she answered pleasantly, "but if you'll excuse me for a minute, I'll talk to one of my colleagues. There may be something we can suggest."

I was grateful to find someone who understood my situation, someone for whom I was not a pariah, but I especially appreciated her welcoming and cordial manner.

"That would indeed be wonderful. Thank you *very* much."

Smiling in response, she disappeared into another room. I waited nervously and excitedly, feeling elated and hopeful, one second, and dejected and weighed down by hopelessness, the next. But there was nothing, I noted cheerlessly, in this quite ordinary storefront office to offer a visual distraction from my inner turmoil.

After about five minutes, she at last returned to the reception area with a noticeable sparkle in her eyes. In fact, she seemed almost gleeful, like an eager co-conspirator.

"The Royal University of Malta!" she exclaimed. "There is a British medical school in Malta. It does accept largely local students, but since you are so advanced in your medical studies, you might apply as a special case—given the political circumstances."

"*Malta?*" I asked. I had no idea where in the world that was.

"Yes," she answered, "it's just southwest of the toe of Italy, below Sicily—the islands of Malta in the Mediterranean. The Royal University accepts new students every two years, but their next round of admissions is scheduled fortuitously for this fall."

My thoughts were swirling in a hundred different directions, I was so excited by the prospect of completing my medical education.

"I will go there and apply immediately," I said.

"I hope that you *will*," she said, with evident enthusiasm.

When I walked back across the piazza and told my compatriots what I'd learned, they seemed nearly as delighted and relieved as I was. We laughed and drank more espresso. As I looked out over the ocean waves once more, they too seemed newly cheerful and buoyant.

All at once, I realized the utter magic of the last half hour. My desperate wish for a solution to my plight, one emerging from the horizon's blue haze, had been answered: my wish had come true!

I would soon set sail toward that very horizon . . . on my way to the Royal University of Malta.

CHAPTER TWO

Szombathely, Hungary
Fall ~ 1938

Lovrana, the small Italian village where my brother and I were now living in exile from our native Austria, was not far from the town of Fiume. Looking through the windows of my train as it rumbled past this town, I could plainly see what I already knew: Fiume had risen into being on both sides of a narrow river and, over the course of time, this river was made to serve as a border that divided the town between two countries. The Italian half was on one side of the river; the Yugoslav half on the other.

But it was a purely superficial divide. Though Fiume and its Yugoslav counterpart, Sushak, had different names and were claimed by different countries, everyone who lived there regarded them as the same town. Crossing the bridge from Fiume into Sushak, it seemed as if my own life was now divided in a similar manner. Everything on one side was part of the life that I lived in Austria. And everything on the other side was part of the life I was living, and would live, in exile. What separated my life into two parts was a fiction, but the results of that fictional divide were all too real.

When my passage to Malta was booked (after half a day spent in search of a freighter sailing not just to Sicily, but to that tiny island country below it, as well), I felt both relieved and reassured. Even though, as I studied a map displayed in one of the shipping offices that I visited, Malta looked as if flung into the Mediterranean by mistake. It appeared to be a small clod of green turf—accidentally launched when the boot that was Italy, kicked the soccer ball that was Sicily, over the salty sea. I noticed that parallels to the enforced uprootedness of my present life were appearing everywhere, perhaps because I felt an overwhelming need to make sense of what was happening to me and those I loved. But, so far, this was impossible.

As I tucked the ticket for my passage to Malta into the recesses of my wallet, I remembered that this smooth leather billfold was a gift from my mother to celebrate my entrance into medical school. Although so much was taken away, at least this small, familiar object was still with me as I entered the next phase of my life, propelled forward by my precious dream of becoming a doctor.

There were now two weeks to wait before setting sail, and I arranged to fill this time by traveling to Hungary—where my intention to marry Lizzie Biró would be formalized with a small engagement party. I was also planning a brief clandestine trip, on my father's behalf, to the town of Czakovec, his birthplace in Yugoslavia.

When my train crossed the bridge from Fiume into Sushak, I was approached and questioned by a plainclothes Yugoslav policeman. He demanded my passport and, after studying it carefully in an expressionless way, confiscated it. During the several hours it took to travel across Yugoslavia, he kept this all-important document in his possession, and did not once allow me out of his sight. When the train stopped at the border of Hungary, this quietly ominous policeman returned my passport without a word, and disappeared into the crowd gathered on the station platform. I tried to put this troubling incident aside and regain my equilibrium by focusing on what made me happiest: medical school and my sweetheart, Lizzie.

The train continued on its way to western Hungary, not far from the Austrian border, where my fiancée and her family resided. This part of Hungary was also where all three of my mother's sisters and their husbands, along with her brother and his wife, made their home. As young boys, my brother, Pauli, and I stayed with several of these families of relatives many times, during the long lazy months of summer. Lizzie and I became childhood playmates then, as her parents were friendly with my Aunt Jenny and Uncle Jenö Bauer. For the few days before and after our engagement party, I was staying with the Bauers in Szombathely again, and I arrived at their home in the early evening on that first day, around dinnertime. As usual, Aunt Jenny asked a great many questions, without bothering to listen to my answers.

"I hear you're planning to finish your medical studies in Malta . . . But what will you do there? You will need to speak English, you know!"

"Well, I think I could learn . . ."

"Why can't they stop that *yelling* out there? Those children have no manners at all, I tell you! But *you*—it's not as if you'll be able to use your Hungarian, or even your German. What does your mother think? I know she's worried sick about you all the time."

"She's all *for* my becoming . . ."

"She's in a bad way at the moment, isn't she? I ought to call her. *Tomorrow*, I'll do that. Would you like more peas? We've grown far too many this year. So eat more, will you? They're good for you!"

My aunt's habit of cutting people off in the middle of an answer used to annoy my brother, Pauli, and me as children, because we were captive, as

My brother, Pauli, (on the left) and me in our sailor suits.
He was then four years old and I was six.

polite boys, to her intrusive chatter. But I was now older by a decade, and I realized it simply escaped her notice that badgering people with questions was socially ungracious. My altered perspective toward an aunt who seemed nearly a kind of nemesis when I was a child startled me. I did not expect my entry into adulthood to be so simple. Was this all it was—a sideways-sliding shift—a new angle from which I perceived things? The apparent fragility of the adult state, made clear by my new realization, was more disturbing to me than my aunt's social ineptitude ever was. If perception alone were the most salient feature of adult life, how did the social fabric hold together?

I long assumed that the realm adults inhabited was in some way solid, or at least possessed a foundation which would not give way. But I saw now that I was naïve: there was nothing solid about it. Everything hinged upon strength of character, and that could easily be weak, at times, or even altogether absent.

The next day, I felt some relief from pondering the puzzling and insubstantial nature of adulthood: Lizzie and I spent many hours together, greatly enjoying each other's company after so long an absence. She looked lovely. We went for a long, strolling walk, holding hands and sharing ardent kisses, both of us feeling immensely happy. These were the nicest hours I experienced in a very long time, but I had yet to do something for my father involving a certain degree of risk.

A cousin of his, who held an important place in the local government of Czakovec, was working on the papers to restore Father's Yugoslav citizenship. But this cousin appeared somewhat lackadaisical, and time was running out. The danger my father faced from the Nazis was imminent. I was determined to visit this cousin and impress upon him the urgent need to complete his part of the repatriation process. To help me accomplish this mission, my Uncle Jenö Bauer found a man who drove a truck across the border into Yugoslavia each day. This man agreed to take me with him if I disguised myself as his assistant.

On the morning of our departure for Czakovec, I woke myself before dawn with a quickly muffled alarm clock, and dressed without light. Taking my breakfast, prepared the night before, from the kitchen ice box, I let myself out the back door. Outside, it was still dark, with a low-lying mist in the distance. I was glad that I brought my jacket, for I soon turned up its collar against the cool morning air. The driver was waiting with his truck full of bricks and building materials when I arrived. "Best not to say much," he cautioned, as we climbed into the truck's cab. "If we're stopped, I'll do the talking for both of us, and you pretend to be a bit slow. Do you know how to grunt?"

I attempted a gruff "UHHNnnn," and he seemed satisfied that I would not put us both in danger by calling attention to myself.

We drove along in the dim pre-dawn light, the truck's headlights revealing the somber, grayish-brown buildings we passed before leaving Szombathely behind us. When the sun came up, color appeared, spreading magnificently over the countryside. The beauty of the fields, fading with a certain melancholy into autumn, penetrated my heart like music. I wished Lizzie could share this moment with me, and perhaps she did. Sometimes it seemed we heard each other's thoughts, and I felt her with me much of the time, even though we were often far apart. We were very much in love.

And very young, I realize now, as both of us felt a buoyant kind of optimism the world had not yet dampened.

In two hours or so, the truck reached the border of Yugoslavia and we passed through without being stopped. I was greatly relieved. The driver gave no outward sign, but some tension in the air of the truck's cab seemed to dissipate. My father's cousin, Andor Hevesy, lived at the top of a hill surrounded by acres and acres of lush vineyards. After the driver and I agreed to meet that evening in the same spot, I trudged up the steep road to my uncle's house.

Since I phoned ahead, Uncle Andor was expecting me. He seemed welcoming enough, perhaps understanding how much fear I felt for my father. Though he did appear a bit embarrassed—probably because of his failure to complete the necessary paperwork—and he repeatedly promised to send the papers off, and forward my father's restored citizenship to Austria, just as soon as it arrived. When I took my leave later that day, I felt certain he was going to keep his promise and my father would be safe.

The trip back to Hungary at dusk seemed to confirm this, since we again passed through the border unquestioned. Everything appeared restored to its former goodness, and the larger forces that disrupted our lives seemed misguided and ineffectual, if not secretly benign.

*   *   *

In the late afternoon, when more mundane affairs could be put aside, we gathered for a small engagement party at the house of my fiancée's parents, the Birós. Half my Hungarian aunts and uncles (the Bauers and Szentes, though not the Löwensteins and Friedrichs), along with Lizzie's parents and her brother, János, all took seats that evening in the Birós' formal dining room. We drank a little local wine, a fine red with a deep, purple-red color. Where chandelier light fell on our wine glasses, the color of the wine was reflected onto the white linen tablecloth, making lovely abstract patterns that danced in the light. Our assembled relatives toasted us, the newly-engaged couple, and offered their congratulations. Some of these toasts were serious and sincere, while others were more lighthearted.

Talk around the table gradually turned to the situation with Germany. Hungarians all, they felt completely safe from Hitler's aggression, his expansionist plans to acquire more *lebenstraum* or "living room" for the German populace. Surely, they agreed with each other, the annexation of Austria was enough for this tyrannical German dictator. No one believed he'd also attempt to seize Hungary.

Conversation then turned to my recent plans for completing my medical education and having Lizzie join me—either in Malta, or when I went to England to practice medicine with my newly earned degree. In between the back-and-forth conversation, Aunt Jenny chattered away about this and that, blithely cutting-off any answers she elicited. But everyone, I noted with interest, responded with equanimity.

Our dinner of hearty Hungarian goulash was not in the least lightened by dessert, a delicious and rich Hungarian chocolate cake served with coffee that perfumed the air with a delightful aroma. All in all, it was a heart-warming evening for me, especially as I'd lately felt deprived of family life and its convivial comfort.

Around the table were several people I'd known nearly my entire life: Aunt Jenny, of course, with her nervous banter, a thin woman with dark hair; beside her, Uncle Jenö, her husband, a tall man who looked exactly like the lawyer he was. Next to him was Aunt Clody, who doted on her little dog, a lively and mop-like white terrier. Her husband, Uncle Lajos Szente, was an architect whose greatest enjoyment came from proudly recalling his military service in World War I (on his wall at home was a pair of crossed sabers, and in his desk drawer, a collection of war medals).

But it was my mother's absent siblings who were truly my family favorites—especially Aunt Paula who, like my mother and grandmother, was warm and friendly. When my brother and I were young, we enjoyed staying with this aunt and her husband, Uncle Ignác Löwenstein, during the summer months. Not least because of their two sons—with whom my brother and I swam in nearby Lake Balaton, and hiked in the alpine foothills—though our older cousins couldn't be more different from one another. Pista, the elder of the two, was tall and serious, a studious sort who later took a degree in agriculture at the University of Halle in Germany. He married a woman who was somewhat unusual, being both a physician and not Jewish. Zoltán, on the other hand, was to my ten-year-old mind fantastic. He was a hugely attractive role model for me, an outgoing and good-looking young man who never studied, who had a great way with women, and who was a natural musician. He could play any piece of music he heard and liked on either the piano or the violin. To entertain us, Zoltán paraded around the room, flailing away with his violin bow for dramatic effect (gypsy music was popular in the local cafés, and my cousin liked to imitate their musical mannerisms).

But Zoltán's musicianship impressed me for another reason, too. I studied piano from an early age, taking lessons twice a week, and was unable to play even a single piece by ear, and certainly not after hearing it just once. Instead, I played in the usual way, practicing musical phrases over and over, until producing them more or less correctly, and progressing from simpler to more complex pieces, as my skill grew. That Zoltán immediately reproduced a tune without benefit of a single lesson, was an astonishing feat. It seemed akin to being a hero—at least, in my estimation.

Almost as fantastic was his ability to be so natural and unaffected around girls. He may have been older by nearly a decade, but I was still impressed by his charm and success. To me, girls still seemed somewhat mysterious, even though I studied them more ardently with each passing year. In time, however, I found my own way to befriend and become close to members of the opposite sex, and now congratulated myself on being engaged to the one woman I truly loved. The thought of our marriage—assured by my new plan to finish my degree in Malta—created a warm glow of happiness and excitement throughout my entire being.

Among the others not present at my engagement party, was Uncle Gusty Friedrich, my mother's brother. He, like her, was a warm person, although fairly simple and lacking in a cultural life, as he had no interest in reading books. When I was younger, this seemed depressing to me, as I spent so much of my time in the good company of books. His wife, my Aunt Aranka, was taller than he and decidedly overweight, while my uncle was quite thin. Aunt Aranka was also very outgoing, while Uncle Gusty was a little too accommodating and unassertive. Their daughter, Edith, took after her mother in both appearance and personality.

For most of each year, our beloved Grandmother Roserl lived with the Friedrich family. Partly, this was because they resided in a small house in a rural village, one quite similar to the Burgenland home where Grandma Rosie raised her five children (the youngest of whom was my mother). The front of the Friedrich's single-story house was occupied by Uncle Gusty's hardware store, which specialized in farming supplies, and the family lived in rooms directly behind the store. Outside was a courtyard, and as was typical in rural life at that time, an outdoor lavatory.

What Grandma Rosie contributed to her son's family life was a calming influence: whatever was problematic in the personality of her daughter-in-law (Aunt Aranka tended to be rather high-strung), Grandma Rosie supplied the antidote with her always-soothing presence. She was a charming natural storyteller, as well, wonderful at creating a sense of family tradition with her delightful stories about long-gone relatives. As children, my brother and I loved hearing her endless and fascinating tales about our distant relations, and how they lived in the "ancient days" of sixty years ago, when Grandma Rosie had been a child, too. A warm and wise matriarch, she was a treasure our family cherished. In fact, her children competed with one another to have the pleasure of her company,

Our beloved family matriarch, Grandma Rosie, seated outdoors,
with my mother, Elserl, perched on the arm of her chair. I am
standing on the left, then a boy of thirteen. My brother, Pauli, sits
crosslegged on the grass in front, with our Cousin Edith beside him.

for she had no home of her own, then, but spent her later years traveling among her children's homes. And as she stayed with the family of each grown child, Grandma Rosie knitted doilies and small blankets. Soon every piece of furniture was covered by her handiwork, and there came a time when no unadorned surface could be found in any of the homes of her children.

Grandma Rosie stayed with our family when we still lived in the house where, on April 19, 1915, I was born. Number 33 Annenstrasse was an undistinguished, three-story row home, set on a busy thoroughfare leading to the railway station in Graz, Austria's second largest city. My parents and I, and my brother Pauli, who was two years younger (though born just five days apart, on the 14th of April), all lived on the second floor. Pauli and I shared a room with a large balcony overlooking a somewhat drab courtyard that was dominated by a flock of white and speckled chickens. The flock's rooster crowed exuberantly each morning, just as the glow of dawn began to define the far edges of the horizon. Beyond the courtyard, there was a grassy field that surrounded a distant factory.

In time, we befriended two other children who played on the balcony next door. By devising games between our balconies, we managed to entertain ourselves in surroundings that were somewhat lacking in things of interest to children.

The first floor of Number 33 housed Herlinger & Deutsch, my father's grain importing firm; there was also a tailor who worked and lived in a separate part of that same floor. My father, Ernst Herlinger, who was born on February 10, 1888, had a serious physical ailment: he was an insulin-dependent diabetic. As a result, he did not engage in actual combat during World War I, but instead served as an officer managing the importation of grain (from the Balkans and Hungary) to feed the Austrian military. When the war ended, he used this experience to establish his own grain importing firm.

My father, Ernst Herlinger, a kind and thoughtful man,
who was an intellectual and a lover of classical music,
as well as a successful businessman.

Father was very knowledgeable about German literature, and he loved to retire after dinner to the superb study in the enormous house we moved to a few years later. Sitting in a comfortable chair, surrounded by his wonderful library of books, he smoked a good cigar while reading his favorite authors: Schiller, Heine, Goethe, and the more contemporary Wassermann. When he was a young man, Father played the classical violin, so he enjoyed taking his family to concerts and the opera. It was he who encouraged my efforts to master the piano. When I practiced well, he enjoyed listening—especially if I were learning a Chopin sonata or Beethoven symphony, or perhaps a piece by Mendelssohn.

While Father was an intellectual, with a naturally more reserved personality than my mother, he nevertheless was a kind man who cared deeply about his family. I still have several letters expressing his love and concern for us all, and for his oldest son, in particular. One of the letters he wrote prior to my journey to Malta concluded with these warm words: "I wish from my heart much success for your future, and the very best results with your studies. With many kisses, from your loving Father."

Grandfather Moritz Herlinger, my father's father, lived with us on the third floor at 33 Annenstrasse. I remember him as dignified and slim, an older gentleman who seemed to enjoy his quietly ruminative life. Like my father, he followed a daily routine that never varied. Every day after lunch, he walked two blocks to a local *kaffeehaus*, using his walking stick to indicate to other pedestrians which direction he was about to take, and in this way avoiding sidewalk collisions. Then Grandfather Moritz had his usual coffee with a little milk, along with a peaceful smoke, while sitting in the coffee shop. His wife, my father's mother, died before I was born, but her sepia-toned photograph in its heavily gilded frame held a place of honor in our home.

Two other people lived with Grandfather Moritz on the third floor: my Aunt Ollie, his daughter, and my other Uncle Andor, his younger son. From time to time, Aunt Ollie's husband, Goldie Kaufman, visited. Uncle Goldie owned a cardboard box factory in Graz, but I never learned what sort of arrangement he and my aunt had, for it came as a surprise to me when, one day, he appeared. I had no idea that Aunt Ollie was married. But as it seemed rude to question the intimate lives of my adult relatives, I never asked how the marriage came about, or when, or why it was conducted in this strange manner. Aunt Ollie *was*, however, an attractive blonde woman, and when she was younger and not yet overweight, she won a beauty contest in Varazdin, a small town in Yugoslavia. Now, her greatest joy seemed to come from sitting on a cushioned seat between her large double windows. From this vantage point, she watched the passing parade on the Annenstrasse, sometimes leaning far out for a better view of an interesting scenario unfolding in the street below.

My Uncle Andor, Father's younger brother, I remember as tall, handsome, and affectionate. When Pauli and I were very little, he picked us up, one by one, to give us bear hugs. This we found delightful. Though his life remains something of a mystery to me, since Andor died in his thirties (and as he converted, at some point, to Catholicism, was buried in the Central Cemetery in Graz, a large Catholic cemetery).

But my relationship with my mother was by far my closest family tie. She was a very young mother, giving birth to me when just eighteen years old, so our ages were not that far apart. She had a very youthful personality,

My mother, Else Friedrich Herlinger, with whom I had a lively and loving friendship, partly because she was only eighteen years older. I never called her Mother, as my brother did, but "Elserl," which meant "Little Elsa."

too, perhaps because she was the youngest child in her family, born just three years before the turn of the century, on September 28, 1897. She loved to laugh and joke light-heartedly with her two young sons, and when I was a teenager of seventeen, and she a youngish mother of thirty-five, Elserl delighted in talking over my relationships with various girlfriends. I don't ever remember calling her "Mother," but always used the name Elserl or "Little Elsa." She, for her part, always called me "Hansikam" or "my little Hans" in her native Hungarian. It was a measure of our affection for each other that we used these nicknames. But our sibling-like closeness was something she and I alone shared, for my brother always addressed her more traditionally as "Mother."

From my perspective as the eldest son, it seemed my parents' marriage was a happy one, even though their differences were not just chronological (Father was nine years Else's senior), but temperamental. He was quite serious and thoughtful, whereas she was almost girlish in sensibility, though she was warm and empathetic as a mother, and took great interest in both her children. My parents did, however, live in different worlds. Father was a businessman who built a successful business and employed a handful of people both at work and at home. Else, for her part, was largely alone during the early years of her marriage when World War I was fought, and Father served in the Austrian Army. When he returned, she gradually transformed into a married woman who managed a large household—one comprised not only of her own family, but of her husband's relatives and, later on, several live-in household staff. So my parents spent their lives in very different pursuits, and my father's joys were not the same as my mother's, and vice versa.

But the accommodations they made to each other served them well, and were common ones within the social climate of that place and time. By way of illustration, I remember something that happened when I was perhaps seven years old. Learning that Father planned to take a brief trip to Italy by himself, I became uncharacteristically and irrationally upset. I have no idea why I behaved this way, but I remember throwing myself on the sofa, in a fit of screaming and crying, and I refused to stop until he agreed to take me with him. Once we arrived, I learned why he wasn't eager to have me along. That evening, we ate dinner with a young woman he seemed very fond of, and all during the meal they behaved as if they knew each other extremely well. When we returned to Graz, I instinctively knew not to mention this young woman to anyone. For his part, Father did not discuss her with me, nor did he ever see the young Italian woman again, as far as I knew.

Perhaps this puzzling incident disappeared without a trace because Father's business was then doing extremely well—so well that, some months later, we moved to a very large house in a more fashionable part of town. Our new house at 41 Elisabethstrasse was almost a mansion. Built in a horseshoe shape, it had two wings and a middle section enclosing a central courtyard. The upper level of this courtyard was graced with a beautiful and symmetrical formal garden. A flight of stone steps descended from the garden to the lower level and its driveway, leading to a large interior garage.

One wing of this house held our parents' bedroom and master bathroom, along with the bedroom and study-music room that Pauli and I shared. The other wing housed the kitchen, laundry, and the storage rooms used by our cook and maid. In the central section, there were two salons, a formal dining room, Father's magnificent study, and a smaller dining room for everyday use. Living quarters for a *portier*, his family, and two service people were located on the ground floor.

We all adjusted quite quickly to our splendid new home, and Father even acquired a second car for our two-car garage. It was a magnificent *Graef und Stift.* Then considered the Rolls Royce of Austria, this grand car was so large that, when it was sold years later, it was converted into an ambulance. But such was the splendor of our new life that even our cook was distinguished. Marie Schober was once the cook and housekeeper for Peter Rosegger, the famous Austrian author and poet who nearly won the Nobel Prize for Literature in 1913 (and received medals of honor from Emperors Wilhelm II and Franz Joseph I, of Germany and Austria, respectively). As a boy of eight or nine, though, I valued Marie chiefly as a steady source of schillings. I knew she was willing to give me the price of a new toy or a book, and that Elserl would always repay whatever amount I "borrowed."

I'm not sure if Pauli discovered this useful banking system or not, but we did share our enthusiasm for a somewhat risky game we invented. It was played on our ground level courtyard with a handful of neighborhood boys,

A formal photograph of me and my brother, Pauli, when I was
thirteen and he eleven years old. Though we were both born in
April, just five days apart, we had very different directions in life.
We did, however, share a love of skiing and swimming.

and we called it "bicycle polo." Using broomsticks as polo mallets, and riding bicycles instead of horses, we careened around the courtyard at top speed, chasing a small rubber ball from one end to the other. The risk came from our degree of daring. We might cut another boy off by blocking his path with our bicycle wheel, hoping to topple him over, or else stick our broomstick through the spokes of another boy's wheel, causing him to fall and suffer defeat. The latter sort of accident is what happened to me: my front wheel became abruptly stationary because of another boy's "polo mallet," and I flew over the handlebars, landing on my wrist. In the hospital, I learned the bones of my wrist were fractured, and that I wasn't allowed to play bicycle polo while waiting weeks for it to heal. Fortunately, I loved books, so it wasn't much of a hardship. Pauli, on the other hand, was a different kind of boy. Except for bicycle polo, hiking, skiing, and swimming, we went our separate ways, and cultivated different friends. Much later, our differences could be seen in our choice of direction in life: Pauli joined my father in business, while I entered medical school. But perhaps our differences were heightened by the fact that my first years of school, unlike my brother's, were ones I spent at home.

My mother's friend, Magda Schmidt, chose as her future husband a quite nice young dentist. But Magda's father disapproved so violently of his daughter's new fiancé that he threw her out of the family home. My mother rescued Magda, and invited her to live with us. But since Magda had a teaching certificate, she agreed to begin my formal education in exchange for room and board. For two full years, Magda and I worked together for several hours each day. She taught me to read and spell, as well as the rudiments of basic mathematics.

Interspersed with my home schooling were piano lessons. Two times each week, my piano teacher came to our house, and for an hour or more, Miss Schulz listened to my practice pieces, corrected my mistakes, and assigned new music. After I studied the piano for seven years, I was invited, along with my teacher's other advanced students, to play a recital in the Stephaniensaal, the main concert hall in Graz. This was a formal and quite scary occasion, and I practiced for it ceaselessly, going over and over each passage of the piece I was to play. Gradually, the notes of the music seemed to flow from my fingers with no conscious thought on my part. My hands memorized their positions, and simply played by themselves.

On the evening of the recital I wore my best suit, a boy of fourteen with my hair slicked back, my hands carefully cleaned, and my nails cut as short as possible, so not to interfere with my playing. Under the bright lights of the stage, as I sat before a Steinway grand piano with its lid raised like the impressive fan of a peacock's tail, I felt a fine mist of sweat spreading across my forehead. Positioning my hands over the keyboard, the way I'd been taught to do, I counted out the beats and began the opening chords. My hands appeared to have a life of their own, flying over the keys with no conscious interference from me. Then I heard applause from the general direction of the audience, swelling slightly in a polite crescendo, and gradually subsiding. I rose, meanwhile, bowed ceremoniously from the waist, and walked off stage into the wings. Much as I loved music, I did not enjoy performing for an audience of adults, and do not believe I was alone in that sentiment!

But if being a student of the piano meant a certain kind of public misery, the student of skiing had almost no audience, if he found himself face-down in a bank of snow, instead of sailing effortlessly down the mountainside. One of my father's employees was an excellent skier, and he was entrusted with the task of giving me skiing lessons when I was not yet ten years old. I can still remember my first lesson. We trudged up a modest hill east of Graz, he attached my skis to my boots, and then I pushed off in a downward direction. Sliding uncertainly between a few trees, I crossed a path and continued over the edge of a frozen brook. Next thing I knew, I fell down hard in a sitting position on a streambed of sharp rocks. It hurt quite a bit so I yelled, and this incident put an end to my skiing lessons. A year or so later, our family spent a few weeks during the Christmas holiday in an area north of our city, a place called the Semmering. There my brother and I enrolled in a real ski school, and were soon descending the slopes with ease.

Some years later, I entered and won an international skiing competition, and my name appeared in the paper. The next day, I was admonished by the administrators of my school. I was using a bogus doctor's excuse to exempt myself "for health reasons" from the tedious exercise machines that all students were required to employ during the winter months. But despite this run-in with authority, I continued to enjoy skiing for much of my life. And I can still smell the crisp, clear scent of Alpine snow, and see it fanning up in the air with a shower of white, when my skis turn sharply, sliding across that powdery softness at just the right angle.

Long before I learned to ski, though, there was another moment of school-related humiliation that I recall most vividly. Facing my first day of the third form (similar to the third grade) in the Evangelical or Christian "Volksschule" in Graz, after being schooled at home for two years, I was taken into a classroom during the math lesson. Then about seven years old, I stood in front of this class with my adult chaperone, while a chorus of students repeated the multiplication tables. "One times six is six," they intoned in rhythmic unison. "Two times six is . . ." When they at last finished their metronomic recitation, I was formally introduced to the whole class, and a given a seat at the back of the room.

Perhaps wanting to make me feel included, the teacher soon instructed me to tell the class what the sum of one hundred times zero would be. As I stood to answer, it seemed to me that, though the answer was probably zero, surely, this teacher wasn't asking a question with zero as the answer—so I offered the next best thing.

"One," I said.

The room burst into uproarious laughter, and the red-faced shame of that experience was with me for quite some time. Luckily, my skills in reading and writing were much better than my mathematical ability, and I was two years younger than the usual age when I passed the entrance examination for the *Realgymnasium*, a kind of middle school. Located within walking distance of our Elisabethstrasse home, it was here that I first studied languages—Latin, French, and English—along with math, physics, and chemistry. Classes were held until four in the afternoon, seven days a week, with the exception of Saturday afternoons. Physical education, always scheduled for the afternoon, included a variety of sports: hand ball, soccer, gymnastics, and, in the winter months, those tedious exercise machines were sometimes interspersed with the far more enjoyable exercise of skating on frozen ponds.

Though the *Realgymnasium* possessed a very good scholastic reputation, expecting a lot from its students academically, there was still time to lead a normal teenage life. And since the Austrian Alps were so close, it was natural to spend our free time hiking and mountain climbing. But on a class trip, one afternoon, a few boys in my class decided to climb a famous cliff known as the *rot wand*, or red wall. I was always fairly fearless, physically, although I was by nature quiet, like my father, and neither socially prone to call attention to myself, nor overly gregarious. Still, the *rot wand* presented a challenge, and I set about attempting to scale it with several classmates.

When I was about ten feet up the face of this cliff, I miscalculated my footing and found myself falling, slipping down past the section of rock I'd just climbed, and landing quite forcefully on the ground below. Fortunately, nothing was broken, though I probably sprained my ankle, as it was very painful to walk. My classmates wanted to create a kind of party from my misfortune, and cheerfully built a stretcher from fallen branches tied together with shirts and jackets. They insisted upon carrying me to a relative's farmhouse in the valley, all the while singing Austrian "wanderer" songs. My father drove over the next day and picked me up.

But I remember that fall from the red cliff as the most "enjoyable" accident I ever experienced.

In the summer months, when school was over for the year, my family many times spent several weeks in Abbazia, the seaside resort town in eastern Italy. Pauli and I loved swimming at the beach in the Gulf of Quarnero. As we got older, we came to love the beach for another reason, as well: it was a place where girls wore bathing suits. In the late 1920s and early 1930s, these were fairly modest garments, but they nevertheless stimulated our adolescent imaginations. This is not to say we understood the intimate mechanics of relations between the sexes; we knew only that we were drawn to girls, and tried to study them surreptitiously, when given the opportunity.

One summer, when I must have been about fifteen, I decided to investigate this matter a little further. Among boys my age, it was well-known that there was a house beyond the forest above the town with a special reputation. Intrepid in the pursuit of knowledge, I one day gathered up all my courage and went there. In my pocket was a small sum of Italian lira, which I understood to be the price of admission. In any case, after being shown into a room, accompanied by a young woman who must have been in her mid-twenties, but who seemed impossibly older and wiser than I was, we exchanged pleasantries. She then quickly established that I didn't really understand what the basic principle of engagement entailed, so she did her best to enlighten me, in a manner that was very kind. After fumbling around for a few minutes, we ended our tryst and I left the house, self-consciously convinced that all who saw my face would know where I had been. As I found the whole thing extremely embarrassing, I never mentioned it to anyone, and certainly not to other boys, for I was hardly able to brag about this awkward encounter.

Once our family returned from Abbazia each summer, Pauli and I usually traveled to Hungary where we'd stay with one or more of our aunts and uncles, for the remainder of the season. As I grew older and entered my mid-teens, my cousin, Zoltán, and I often visited the cafés at night to listen to gypsies. They earned a living by playing their lively folk music in the local establishments. Then, the summer always came to an end, and we returned to our studies in Graz. By the time I was eighteen, I progressed from the "prima" to the "octava" forms in the *Realgymnasium*, and was ready to study for the matriculating exams required to enter the university. In 1933, when I passed those entrance exams, I was accepted by the Karl Franzen's University in Graz. Disturbingly, in January of that same year, Hitler became the Chancellor of Germany.

*   *   *

The engagement party at the Birós' house was coming to a close. Lizzie and I accepted more congratulations, thanking everyone for coming. We then hastily agreed that she would visit me before I sailed for Malta. We kissed good night, and I returned with the Bauers to stay at their house before leaving early the next morning for Italy.

As my train crossed the bridge over the narrow river dividing Yugoslavia from Italy once more, it struck me that these divisions between two countries—between two quite familiar-to-each-other groups of people—were worse than foolish. My family held within its arms such human variety, yet all of us were members of the same family. A good family, it seemed to me. I asked myself what it was about the perspective of adults that made these divisions seem desirable and even necessary, but I found this impossible to fathom.

Once back in Lovrana, there were only a few days left before my ship sailed for Malta. The next day, I arranged to meet Lizzie and her brother in Abbazia, expecting their visit to occupy me until then. Pauli and I packed our belongings, and then traveled by bus to that resort so familiar to us as the setting for our family vacations.

In the morning, we went off to meet my fiancée and her brother at the train station. Since it was located on a hilltop overlooking the town and the vast sparkling sea, the four of us—in a festive mood— hired a horse-drawn carriage for the trip back down to our hotel. Our several days together were spent sunning ourselves and swimming, dressing for dinner, and dancing into the night, as stars appeared in the dark sky, and the evening air was refreshed by a gentle offshore breeze. One early evening, as we were walking to dinner together, we passed a street photographer. Lizzie wanted a photograph. We had one made, and I have it still. In this postcard picture, all four of us are striding along. I am on the right, with Lizzie walking next to me, an attractive young woman dressed in stylish trousers. Next to her is Pauli, then János, a tall fellow on the left. Lizzie and János are smiling, while Pauli and I are more somber. Perhaps this reflects the greater dismay my brother and I had faced, concerning the fate of our family and ourselves, while Lizzie and János had not yet felt personally affected by the ominous air of events in Europe. Whatever the reason, we were together in that brief moment in time, captured by a street photographer.

*Just before I sailed for the Royal University in Malta in 1938,
this picture was taken by a street vendor in Abbazia, Italy. I am
on the right, Lizzie, my fiancée, is beside me. My brother, Pauli,
is next, with János, Lizzie's brother, on the left.*

A day or so before I left for our brief holiday in Abbazia, I received a letter from Father. He was told of my last-minute efforts to hasten his Yugoslav citizenship, and so he wrote, "I do not doubt that, with our combined efforts, it may be possible to master our fate, and achieve a home where we may, once again, live together happily and in peace."

∞

CHAPTER THREE

Valletta, Malta
Fall, 1938 ~ Winter, 1940

The cargo ship on which I'd booked my passage to Malta would soon set sail from the harbor town of Genoa on Italy's western coast. But as the bus that would take me to Genoa made its way across Italy's geographical boot top, meandering ever closer to my destination, I found myself unable to relax—even though my journey lasted from the middle of the morning until late in the afternoon. When we at last entered the bus depot in Genoa, my nervous anticipation began to drain away. I gathered up my luggage and found my way to the harbor overlooking the Ligurian Sea. Along this same coast, to the west of Genoa, lay the French Riviera and the Cote d'Azur. But I would be sailing south—down Italy's long coastline—before slipping over the toe of her boot, then rounding the eastern edge of Sicily to disembark on Malta. The Maltese Islands, an archipelago of three small islands (Malta, Camino, Gozo), lay southwest of the far larger Sicilian land mass to the north.

By late afternoon, I handed my ticket to the captain of the Maria del Mare, and was directed to a cabin on the upper deck. Though primarily a freighter, the Maria was outfitted to accommodate a dozen or so passengers. And my cabin was quite adequate for the single week I would be at sea, boasting a porthole window the color of pewter, and through it a glimpse of other boats docked in the harbor. The buildings of Genoa were visible in the far background.

I placed my bags—the same heavy suitcases I brought with me from Graz—on the bunkbed's lower berth, then checked the bedding on the upper mattress. Since the night air was cooler, now, I removed the blanket from the foot of the bottom bed and spread it across mine. I tucked in two of its corners as I stood on the sturdy metal bedframe. After washing up from my journey in the cabin's small lavatory, I joined the other passengers waiting for dinner on the back deck, where enticing aromas from the galley kitchen wafted by.

Among those gathered in the twilight were several businessmen and as many tourists, along with a few whose reason for travel I could not discern. Most were leaning on the ship's railing, looking past the harbor toward the distant horizon. As I gazed with them out over the water, I was reminded of the hazy horizon at Trieste, and the astounding luck that brought me here to this ship bound for Malta.

My life might lack a firm footing, but another sort of footing had materialized, courtesy of magical circumstances. "Mastering our fate," as Father phrased it, did indeed seem possible if such circumstances reliably appeared, whenever our path in life was blocked by an insurmountable impasse. It then seemed to me a good sign when I suddenly felt both hungry and tired. At some point during the previous hours, my faith that things were going to go as planned was restored. I did not doubt that I was really here, on this ship, with my departure for Malta imminent.

At dinner, that evening, I became nominally acquainted with the other passengers, most of whom were middle-aged, with the exception of one young woman of about twenty, accompanied by her mother. On holiday from the German city of Munich, Johanna and her mother, Frau Stein, appeared pleased to find someone with whom they could conduct a pleasant conversation. Johanna was especially relieved, she told me, to find a peer. Actually, she confided, she was delighted, because the entire ship was filled with people around her mother's age, which was quite dreadfully old. "*Sie ist*," she repeated with mock chagrin, "*sehr alt*."

After a simple but plentiful Italian dinner of *penne y pesci*, pasta with fish, served with many glasses of welcome Chianti, I went out on the deck for a smoke. It was then I realized that the Maria had pulled away from her berth beside the dock, and was steaming slowly out of the harbor. As I stood there smoking happily, while delighting in the lonely ship lights reflected on the dark water, we began to pick up speed. The intoxicating scent of sea air came to me more forcefully, then, as a mist of seawater spraying upwards from the ship's bow blew back against my face. In a little while, I began to wish that I might, through the sheer force of my longing, bring Lizzie to this ship to stand with me under the stars. When I later fell asleep in a collapse of nervous exhaustion, I felt both happy and immensely hopeful that all my difficulties were now past.

Several days later, we stopped for twenty-four hours in the Rome seaport of Ostia and were able to go ashore. Frau Stein and Johanna were glad that I squired them around, as my Italian was slightly more assured than theirs, and they wished to find several small gifts for family members and friends. We walked and walked, with many leisurely hours on land to fill, while the Maria offloaded half her cargo and took on new freight.

During our day of shopping and sightseeing, we decided to visit the Vatican in St. Peter's Square. Johanna had never experienced these enormously large and graceful buildings with their Bernini columns, and the Sistine Chapel's treasured Michelangelo frescoes and sculpture. We did not have time to do these magnificent buildings justice, but I was moved all the same, as if I were seeing them for the first time. As we were leaving, my gaze followed the flight of several pigeons gliding gracefully over the fountains in St. Peter's Square, before circling the tall Eqyptian obelisk at its center. The square reminded me of the grandeur of public buildings in Austria, especially those in Graz and Vienna. It was then I remembered an article I'd read several years earlier in the *Tagespost*, Graz's daily newspaper. The young Adolf Hitler's love of painting the Vienna Opera House was described in detail, along with the fact that he was twice rejected by the Vienna Academy of Fine Arts. Unable to achieve recognition as an artist, Hitler decided to make his mark as a politician. But he sadly became a politician who seized upon the anti-Semitism long fermenting on the conservative fringes of Viennese politics. This factional undercurrent was largely interested in dehumanizing Austrian Jews, making us a convenient scapegoat for every social and economic problem imaginable. These thoughts angered me, but I tried to put them aside, in order to help Johanna choose among three or four possible gifts for her brother, Heinz. He was, she explained, exactly my age. Toward late afternoon, we made our way back to the dock and boarded our freighter, knowing a dinner of fresh fish with a medley of local foods—feta cheese, and the olives, tomatoes, and zucchini displayed in the seaside market— was waiting.

During the rest of our week of travel, the Maria stopped at several other ports of call, among them Naples and, when we reached Sicily, Messina and Siracuse. Just before dawn on my last morning at sea, I woke and saw a dark silhouette on the horizon. Half asleep, I watched it grow gradually larger in my cabin's porthole window, before realizing it was the island of Malta. Hurriedly, I flung myself out of bed, shaved and dressed, and since I packed almost everything the night before, presented myself a few minutes later on deck. Only a few passengers were disembarking at Valletta. Johanna and her mother would remain on board as the Maria turned back and sailed north, making her way up the eastern coast of Italy.

The Steins and I said our final goodbyes on deck, standing in the morning fog. I thanked them for their congenial company during our onshore adventures in Italy and Sicily, but I did not expect to ever see them again. We waved goodbye and they turned away, heading for their home in Munich.

*   *   *

Standing with two suitcases at my feet, my excitement about finally arriving in Malta made me also a little anxious, and as I watched a Maltese policeman check the passports of our small group of disembarking passengers, I felt a flash of fear. What if this policeman prevented me from entering the island, despite the fact that, since the early 1800s, it was subject to Britain's colonial rule? Glancing casually at the stamp of Austrian citizenship in my passport, he handed back the little leather book and politely answered my question about nearby hotels. Walking away in search of accommodation, weighed down by my cumbersome suitcases, I felt relieved by this small reprieve from further calamity and worry. I checked into the first ancient hotel I happened across and, leaving my room almost immediately, walked down a brief corridor, descended some steeply narrow interior stairs, and found my way outside again. I was eager to explore my new home. While following the winding street that led away from my hotel, I realized Valletta was built on a narrow peninsula of land that jutted into a wide harbor, carved from the middle of the island. This peninsula pointed in a northeasterly direction, and was threaded along its highest point by Valletta's main street. Several parallel streets traversed the peninsula's lower levels, and many side streets branched off from these lower-level streets, leading down steep hills to the sea. And, as I noticed somewhat later during my Maltese days, when the sky was clear and the sun brilliant overhead, it was possible to see the cratered, snow-capped top of Mt. Aetna, the famous volcano in Sicily. It was a lovely and awe-inspiring sight, and somewhat appeased the homesickness I felt for my Austrian Alps.

The next morning, I gathered the documentation from my years of medical school in Graz, and presented myself at the office of the Secretary of the Royal University of Malta. Like most things in this island country known for Neolithic temple ruins dating from 6,000 B.C. (they were thought to be the oldest in the world), the University, too, had an exceedingly long and venerable past. It was founded by Jesuits as the Collegium Melitense in 1592, and its college of medicine was established nearly a hundred years later, in 1676. After a brief wait in the anteroom, I was introduced to the University secretary, a Mr. Pace, and we sat in the comfortable, well-aged ambience of his office. I explained my desire to be admitted, "Because," I found myself concluding with some feeling, it represented "my only remaining hope." And, indeed, it did.

"I must say, Mr. Herlinger," began Mr. Pace, in response, "that yours is a most unusual application. We have never, in my memory, received another one like it. But I can certainly sympathize with your predicament."

He then paused briefly before continuing, "And I will submit your paperwork to the Council, asking them to hasten their decision. You may expect to hear from me within a few days."

I assured Mr. Pace—a patient man with graying hair, a moustache, and thick eyebrows—that I was going to pay my own way. Several of my uncles agreed to fund this final period of my medical education (since my father's business suffered a reversal when the bank he depended upon failed, forcing our family to move back to 33 Annenstrasse, just before I was exiled). I also told Mr. Pace that I hoped to repay England for granting my degree, by joining the British Colonial Services after graduation. He replied that this was all well and good, furthering my petition with the governing board of the medical school.

As promised, Mr. Pace called me into his office within the week to meet with the Chairman of the Medical Faculty. The chairman fairly quickly became convinced of my legitimate status as a medical student and, without further ado, I was invited to join the final year class. Both men did inform me that I would need to repeat some of the examinations I had

*My Royal University student I.D. photo, a document on thin,
gray-green paper that now seems impossibly fragile, though it has
survived for sixty-seven years. In Malta I could complete my
medical degree at a school whose certification would be
recognized by England and, therefore, the world.*

already taken in Graz. As these were going to be administered in English, they suggested I find a tutor to gain better mastery of the language, particularly with regard to medical terminology. This I was quite willing and eager to do.

Meanwhile, I received a letter from my brother, Pauli, telling me that he'd traveled to Haifa in Palestine. There he applied to the Technicon, the technical university, taking a job in a coffee house to support himself. Lizzie, too, sent a letter. She missed me, she wrote, and hoped I succeeded in entering the medical college. I'd written her several times about my adventures while traveling to Malta, though it was with some sadness that I realized our engagement party seemed a long time ago. The dust of a mild estrangement seemed to have fallen between us, partly because my attention was now directed toward adjusting to life in a novel Mediterranean culture, one completely encased within British colonial conventions.

But my struggles to acclimate did not go unnoticed. Mr. Pace took it upon himself to inform the Archbishop of Malta about my arrival at the Royal University. The Archbishop assigned Father Laspina, a young

Jesuit, to look after me. Father Laspina was, in every sense of the word, a Godsend, and his presence in my life later became the inspiration for a lifelong transformation. First, though, he improved my mundane worldly affairs by locating an inexpensive flat for me to live in. It was situated on a street running perpendicular to both the *Strada Stretta*, or narrow street, and Valletta's main street. And while it was largely deprived of sunlight, my new apartment had a sitting room, bedroom, kitchen, and bath, and was a big improvement over my single room at the hotel. Father Laspina also arranged for the part-time cleaning services of two young women who worked in a nearby shop selling groceries. He even told me about a restaurant where I might eat a simple spaghetti lunch each day, for the miniscule price of one shilling. Not long thereafter, the small table in the sitting room of my Maltese flat became the center of my world. It was here I studied late into the night, after attending medical lectures in the morning, and working on the wards of the Royal University's hospital in the afternoon and early evening.

In time, I was no longer deprived of female company. There were several university students I dated in a completely chaste way, since Malta was a decidedly Catholic country, and its young women were mindful of certain strictures. This was not the case, however, with the two young women who cleaned my rooms. We struck up an easy familiarity with each other, and they gladly provided a form of physical comfort I was not able to obtain elsewhere. It sometimes amused me to realize that the local prostitutes, who occupied one end of the *Strada Reale*, or King Street, in an area populated by bars and pubs, now accepted me as a local person, and no longer sent their colorful solicitations my way.

The final year class of medical students that I joined at the Royal University numbered only twenty or so, but they were all friendly Maltese, and I soon counted many new acquaintances, along with two real friends. Tom Shockledge was a tall, round-faced fellow, and we got into the habit of swimming together in the sea at Sliema, a small town west of Valletta, after our hours of work on the hospital wards. Another good classmate friend, James Mercieca, who happened to be the son of the Chief Justice of Malta, invited me to have dinner with his family several times. But it was Father Laspina who made the biggest impression. He changed my life for the better, in a totally unforeseen but lasting way. In the first place, he was not a solemn and pedantically pious priest, but a wonderfully active man in his thirties. He loved to play soccer and did so with some difficulty, by hitching up his priestly robe or "soutana" and securing it around his waist. Father Laspina was an avid and enthusiastic walker, as well, and he and I went on long walking tours together, exploring the hilly parts of the old capital, and climbing the dramatic limestone cliffs on the western end of the island. During these walks and climbs, which reminded me of hiking in Austria, his cheerful sense of humor was always in evidence. It served him well as the director of *Actione Catholica*, a Catholic youth organization that offered table tennis, social events, and lectures that were only indirectly concerned with religious matters. Father Laspina invited me to frequent the *Actione Catholica*, realizing I was in need of a social life, as my social ties were quite limited during my first few weeks on Malta. I did wander into the *Actione* quite often, for it was located only a few buildings away from my apartment.

Around this time, I started attending services at the Cathedral of St. John. I found it heartening that I understood the Latin spoken during the Mass (unlike the incomprehensible Hebrew the Rabbi of Graz wanted me to learn as a child). Above all, I felt very welcomed by the Catholicism Father Laspina embodied, and wanted to become part of this friendly religious community. Gradually, after I'd attended services at the Cathedral for several months, I learned how to pray. This opened in me a wholly new feeling of belonging and security, so I felt moved to ask Father Laspina if he'd baptize me. He performed the ceremony beautifully, and I have never regretted this decision, but have been faithful to the Catholicism Father Laspina practiced, ever since.

For me, being Jewish had little to do with religion. There was no religious community in Graz that I felt a part of (my family attended the synagogue on infrequent occasions), so my experience of Judaism was basically a non-experience. Though I'd never deny my Jewish heritage, and insist that every person's beliefs, whatever his or her religious background, be respected. But Father Laspina's Catholicism was a kind of home for me, at a time when I'd lost my family home, and my future seemed fraught with troubling uncertainties. For the peace of belonging that came to me when I prayed, and the security of my connection to the Catholic community on Malta, I remained throughout my life deeply grateful.

Toward the end of that year, I was officially notified that I might sit for the final examinations leading to the degree of Doctor of Medicine. Soon thereafter, I passed the introductory "Rigorosum" exams which I'd already taken in Graz, though I passed them this time in English. I worked hard to improve my usage and understanding of this language, and greatly benefited from the kind help of my English-speaking colleagues, but I still needed to make use of a German-English dictionary. Once my preliminary exams were out of the way, I faced one last hurdle: a broad group of final examinations on such clinical subjects as histology, pathology, and internal medicine, all part of my final year of medical classes on Malta.

During these months of study, hospital work, and new friendships, I kept my parents informed of my progress, and received their letters in return. Then, one morning in late winter, I slit open the tissue-thin sheet of an airmail letter from my mother. It contained terrible news. She wrote that Father, having heard the Nazis were about to make a new round of arrests among influential Jews in Graz, decided to evade them by hiding in the nearby foothills. It was a plan made in desperation and not well-thought-out (Father assumed that the repatriation papers would arrive momentarily, and he and my mother would immigrate to Yugoslavia where they would be safe). After several nights in the cold hills, Father was forced to return home, where the Nazis found and arrested him. He was shipped off, with a group of other men from Graz, to the concentration camp in Dachau, located near Munich, Germany. Within days, since Father was now deprived of his insulin shots, he became disoriented and failed to respond when a Nazi guard shouted an order. Shot with a hand pistol, Father collapsed on the cold winter ground where he stood.

Elserl would not have known about Father's fate, and might never have known, were it not for the fact that two men were kind enough to find her and describe his murder, once they were released from Dachau. For Elserl, it was a loss nothing could assuage. Bleak despair and heartbreak became the husband who accompanied her when she immigrated to Yugoslavia—for the naturalization papers had at last arrived, though they were several weeks too late to save Ernst Herlinger.

*   *   *

During the mid-1970s, thirty years after Father's murder by the Nazis, I visited Munich as a speaker at a medical conference. As soon as I could get away, I took the train to Dachau. Once there, I found no sign of the concentration camp where my father perished. The town's tree-lined residential area was dotted with small shops, businesses, and a few older public buildings, but that was all. When I finally questioned a policeman about the whereabouts of the *Konzentrationslager*, he reluctantly pointed to a row of houses. I saw something then that was invisible to me before: a kind of opening and, further in, a gate. Walking over, I found my way inside, and saw many barracks-type buildings surrounded by empty grounds. As I walked, the sight of these low buildings grew increasingly painful. Images of Father as I'd known him during my childhood appeared in my mind's eye, and I forced myself to imagine what his death must have been like—being shot, for no earthly reason, by strangers whose motives were completely insane. I continued to walk the grounds until I saw every single room and cubicle, every last nook and cranny. And the searing pain I was feeling seemed the least that I could suffer, given Father's pointless murder, and the suffering and deaths of so many others.

After a few hours, I was vaguely aware of a bell sounding in the background. But I ignored it. Then, a guard came to inform me that they were closing for the night. Other than this uniformed man, I'd seen no one else the entire time.

"I have . . . **not** . . . finished," I told the guard in an extremely controlled way, feeling all my pain and rage converge within the timbre of my voice.

The guard appeared startled, even a bit frightened.

"I'm not finished," I repeated, in a more normal tone. "I will take . . . another while."

"Oh. Well. Take your time," he said, his earlier brusque officiousness completely gone. Then he scuttled off somewhere, and did not return.

*   *   *

During my first weeks on Malta, after enrolling at the Royal University, I visited the German consulate and obediently turned over my passport. With the German annexation of Austria during the previous spring, my citizenship was transferred to Germany. Much later, I realized that my passport was now stamped with a "J," a mark identifying me as a Jew— someone Germany would want to claim only for the sake of consignment to a concentration camp. Even so, when England and France together declared war against Germany on September 3, 1939, two days after Nazi forces invaded Poland, I was designated an "enemy alien" by England, the country under whose colonial rule Malta then was. So I now stood—to use that proverbial phrase—"between a rock and a hard place," and faced yet another insurmountable impasse blocking my life's path.

If I added my conversion to Catholicism to these entangled official positions, efforts by warring countries to classify me appeared even *more* mired in absurdity. This was an effect best seen by the way such classifications were completely ignored, in those years, by people who treated me the way we all deserve to be treated: as a fellow human being.

There remains one final incident which helps underscore the essentially farcical nature of all efforts to categorize one group of people or another as sub-human.

When I was in medical school in Graz, I developed a recurring skin irritation for which the best treatment was circumcision. This minor operation was performed by a medical school surgeon whose political views were sympathetic to Nazism, but who felt no antipathy toward me, personally. That I was finally given my *bris*, the Jewish ritual circumcision, by a Nazi, is somehow telling. In its odd way, it reveals how our deep similarities as human beings far outweigh any illusory differences—that politically motivated classifications would try to imprison us within. People are just people, as most of us realize.

But when one group is made sub-human by another, it is almost always an attempt to grab some sort of unearned power. The "-ism" then used to justify that theft will predictably also serve to camouflage its adherents' aggression. From that point on, this same "ism" swiftly becomes a form of self-righteous blind denial, making any mundane theft of power seem instead like an exalted quest.

But despite the fact that the ruses Nazism wore now appear as easily identified as their uniforms, the world was still forced to contend with the terrible results of such fanatic power-seeking—during all the years that this most devastating of wars raged.

And so, in the first days of their country's newly declared war on Germany, the British authorities on Malta scanned the local population and arrested all the foreigners, along with anyone else they suspected of some marginal alignment with the enemy. Because of my Austrian-German passport, I was picked up with about two dozen others, and taken to the local prison, the Fortezza St. Angelo. This fortress, built in the fourteenth century, was perched on the other side of the Grand Harbor, overlooking the sea. My fellow prisoners included assorted Jewish refugees; Maltese intelligentsia who spoke only Italian (their politics were therefore in question, as Italy under Mussolini had become a German ally in May of 1939); Maltese citizens who were simply not trusted; and Maltese citizens of German birth. Among the latter were Herr Mueller, the German consul, a stout Bavarian who loved his beer, and Herr Gegg, the decidedly non-Nazi German who was the chief brewer of Malta, and with whom I developed a close friendship. Herr Gegg was not only a decent sort, he seemed very familiar to me. We shared a similar cultural background, even though he was twice my age. I was friendly, too—though it was thoroughly ironic—with Herr Mueller, the German consul who stamped my passport with a "J." As befits those who find themselves thrown together in odd circumstances, we cultivated a cheerful camaraderie among ourselves, keeping our spirits up with a sense of humor that was very Maltese in flavor. Our evenings, meanwhile, were spent in a very unprison-like way: socializing together in a large room where beer and wine were readily available.

An informal photograph showing all those who, at the start of the war, were arrested by the British on Malta. I am standing in the back row on the far right, the only man wearing a light-colored suit jacket. My friend, Herr Gegg, is standing just below me on the right. His attractive wife is standing to the left of me, just below a man in a uniform and hat. Imprisoned for months in the Fortezza d'Angelo, we cultivated a good-natured camaraderie among ourselves—all of us foreigners to the British, or else Maltese they distrusted.

After a few weeks of confinement (during which time the Italian Air Force sporadically dropped bombs that did very little damage, since the British were successful in keeping the Italian bombers at bay), the British commandant allowed me to return to my studies at the Royal University each morning. After traveling by bus around the curving sweep of the Grand Harbor, I resumed my former routine, attending lectures and working in the hospital, before returning to the ancient fortress in the late afternoon.

After a month and a half spent commuting to the University in this way, I was told that I might leave the prison altogether. This presented a bit of a problem, as I was forced to drop the lease on my small flat when I went off to prison, and apartments were not so readily available now.

Herr Gegg came to my rescue by suggesting that I stay with his family and "look after things," since he was among those forced to remain a prisoner. Gegg's home was in Sliema, the small town west of Valletta where my friend, Tom Shockledge, and I enjoyed our late afternoon swims.

Though I accepted the offer of a place to stay, I was concerned about not taxing the hospitality of Herr Gegg's wife and daughter. In fact, I had every intention of finding a place of my own. But, in a little while, I had no real reason to leave. I enjoyed living in this household, and was quite taken with Frau Gegg's beautiful blue eyes, framed dramatically by her dark hair. Of course, I took pains to conceal this infatuation, feeling constrained by gentlemanly good manners. Unfortunately, my friendship with these charming Germans probably counted against me when the British Secret Service documented my case later on.

For the rest of that year, we lived in a kind of "suspended animation," caught between relative local peace on the island, and the imminent threat of war in Europe. Listening to the radio, we picked up broadcasts from Italy and England, and were sickened by the worsening conditions. After Poland, Hitler toppled Czechoslovakia during the following spring. Then, in January of 1940, our state of semi-peace and semi-war on Malta came to an end. The German *Luftwaffe* took over the Italian air bases in Sicily, and the Germans began bombing the island very heavily, many times each day. The British responded by arresting me again, along with many others—even incarcerating the Chief Justice of Malta (whose son, James Mercieca, I befriended in medical school), because the judge was considered "unreliable" by the authorities.

Life inside the fortress was far more unpredictable this time around. When air raid sirens wailed, since there were no bomb shelters, we took refuge inside the eight-foot-thick walls of the fortress's enormous windows. To reach them, we climbed ladders reaching several feet from the floor of our dormitory rooms. On one such occasion, I stopped to search for a cigarette before climbing into a window. A bomb landed in the courtyard outside, just then, and I was lifted by the explosion and flung completely across the room. Luckily, I was unhurt, except for a few bruises. But never again did I dally, even for a second, when the sirens sounded!

The British, meanwhile, were struggling to contend with the crushing German onslaught and decided to evacuate all their foreign prisoners. We were told to place our packed belongings in one area of the fortress; they were about to load us and everything we owned on the Amakura, a ship waiting in the Grand Harbor. This ship was familiar to us, as it regularly traveled to Valletta from the Sicilian city of Siracuse. Once we boarded the Amakura, all the married men were joined by their families. And I knew my year and some months on Malta were now at an uncertain end.

We set sail for Alexandria in Egypt the same day, spending that night in the desert and sleeping in tents. The next day, we were loaded onto trucks, crossed the Suez Canal, and traveled on to Palestine. The Geggs and all the other interned families were taken to a Palestinian camp at the site of a former German village. But the single men were placed in an internment camp north of Haifa, situated on another peninsula jutting into the Mediterranean Sea. Once we were all "processed," the Jewish refugees among us were released to take up settlement in Palestine. But I was not released, and no reason was provided. When I discussed this by phone with Pauli (my brother was now living in Haifa), he found a lawyer to visit me in the camp and discuss my release through legal means. But I was not entirely certain that gaining my freedom was the best choice. If I became a Palestinian citizen, I was afraid the implicit promise the British authorities had made—to return me to Malta once the Germans were defeated—might simply evaporate.

But the attorney my brother sent informed me that he required payment before taking legal action, and since I then possessed barely enough money to buy cigarettes, I was unable to afford his services. Years later, I learned that my brother not only paid this lawyer's fee in advance, he told Pauli that I "didn't wish to be released"—even though I said nothing whatsoever to him about my fears.

In retrospect, it seems as if magical circumstances intervened on my behalf once more. Were I released, my medical degree surely would have been forfeited. And, partly because I sensed this possibility, I was content to stay put. Besides, like many others, I believed the war could not last much longer.

CHAPTER FOUR

Haifa, Palestine
Entebbe, Uganda
Winter, 1940 ~ Winter, 1945

After resigning myself to an internment in Haifa with no foreseeable end, I set about making the best of my situation. I offered my services to our camp doctor, an Arab physician with a local practice, as volunteering meant I might justifiably spend hours each day in the medical assistance hut. This small wooden structure was situated between two long buildings that housed our sleeping quarters, and though primitive, it proved adequate for performing simple diagnostic tests. After several months spent working under its low ceiling—conducting studies using blood, urine, and stool samples—I became so familiar with our patients' ailments (most commonly, malaria, Dengue Fever, and amoebiasis), that I wrote out a list of the lab materials and medications we lacked, and requested them through the camp commandant. When I later received these supplies, our basic medical capabilities were greatly improved.

Medical pursuits aside, the atmosphere of the camp itself was relatively bleak. Barbed wire fenced us in, and guard towers stood watch over a desert landscape, made inhospitable by frequent sandstorms. Daily life passed by in a blur, with one day scarcely distinguishable from another. The only real novelty occurred when illegal Eastern European immigrants were processed through our camp. Then, the main areas were populated for a short time by several dozen colorful people, who reminded me of peasant farmers or gypsies. Though it might easily be said that the Haifa internees were a rather colorful assemblage of men to begin with; our only common denominator was that we were foreigners to the British.

And this was why it was something of a relief to one day make the acquaintance of a professor of physics from Germany. At twenty-five, I was just slightly older than his former students, which encouraged him, a displaced physicist, to slip into his professorial role. To my delight, Herr Schmidt began teaching me the laws of physics that governed the movement of the stars, the ebb and flow of the ocean tides, and the formation of waves. His explanations were of particular interest in that setting, because the stars were very bright and lovely over the Mediterranean. As we spent hours gazing up at them together, he held forth on the way the stars moved nomadically around the night sky, in concert with the changing seasons.

But his discourse on the rise and fall of ocean tides was of personal interest to me, since the younger internees, myself included, had organized swimming competitions. These we held in a semi-enclosed area, protected from the rougher waves of the open sea by a line of smooth rocks, protruding above the water not far from shore. Later on, we developed another outlet for our pent-up physical energies: fierce soccer matches that we played near the shoreline. When a defensive kick was too strenuously made, one of us jumped into the water to retrieve the ball, and this was always a bit easier when the tide was at its ebb—something I now understood the governing physics of, thanks to my professorial friend.

Despite the surface calm of camp life, we felt the pervasive foreboding the war produced. It seemed to spread in a virus-like fashion among the populations of adjoining countries. In the Haifa camp, our underlying fears grew especially virulent, once we learned that Axis troops were advancing into the Tripoli area of Lebanon, just one hundred and fifty-five miles north. Since that distance was only about a day and a half away by convoy, it was horrible to contemplate. Capture by the Nazis or their Axis allies, Italy and Japan, likely meant death on the spot, or else the slow death of imprisonment in a German concentration camp. The silent dread with which this news colored our feelings and thoughts was heightened by the subsequent movement of German troops into Syria, a mere sixty-two miles away.

The following year, in the summer of 1941, the British became sufficiently disturbed by the proximity of enemy forces to relocate us completely. We were told to pack all our belongings again, what little we then possessed, and just before boarding a relocation train bound for Egypt, I managed to write a brief note to my brother, Pauli. He was living in Tel Aviv, working in a furniture store, and making plans to marry a young woman named Margo, a native of Palestine. I wrote to tell him that I was being deported once more, this time to the British territories of Africa.

Our train traveled west from Palestine, on the Mediterranean edge of the Syrian Desert, and crossed the Suez Canal into Egypt. There we boarded a small ship and sailed, that same night, into the Gulf of Suez. Sailing further south the next day, we entered the Red Sea, which led us into the Gulf of Aden, several days later. In less than a week, the immense continent of Africa appeared in the distance. After one more week at sea, we rounded the Great Horn of Africa (on my map, this famous geographical feature seemed shaped like a rhinoceros' face and horns), and from there we sailed south, past the shoreline of Somalia. When we'd traveled for a little over two weeks, our boat landed at the port of Mombasa. "The aspect of Mombasa," wrote Winston Churchill in his youth, "as she rises from the sea is alluring, even delicious." My own youthful feelings upon seeing Mombasa, a major port for the African country of Kenya, were not as rapturously metaphoric. Like all the other passengers, I was simply relieved to be on land again, after so many days on the pitching seas.

In Mombasa, we boarded a slow-moving train heading west-northwest to the Kenyan capital of Nairobi, a city in which Nubians, Somalis, Arabs, Indians, Pakistanis, and Europeans lived side by side, in jostling international community. Nairobi was long a favorite point of departure for recreational hunters, who were on their way to the Kenyan game lands. But the war diminished "big game" hunting's popularity. This seemed to me fortunate for the lions, leopards, elephants, rhinoceroses, and African buffaloes, with whom I felt a certain comradely sympathy, given the situation my family shared with so many others, as targets of Nazi anti-Semitism.

We were now just south of the Equator, and yet the snow-capped sight of Mt. Kenya, the second highest African peak after Mt. Kilimanjaro, was visible in the distance as we chugged along, eventually crossing the Kenyan border to enter the country of Uganda. Family groups of internees, including my German friends, the Geggs, were placed in another German agricultural settlement. But single men like myself were transported to a British camp in the lake area of Northern Uganda.

As an assistant to the camp's medical officer (I am seated, wearing a white lab coat and stethoscope) in the Soroti internment camp in Uganda, Africa, I visited village clinics run by the British to serve the medical needs of Ugandan mothers and children.

After settling into a camp near Soroti, I again filled my time by practicing medicine. Each morning, I accompanied our camp medical officer on visits to the child and maternity welfare clinics which the British established in the surrounding villages. The Ugandans seemed for the most part healthy and well-fed, their diet consisting of grains, plantain, cassava (a starchy root plant that resembled a potato), nutritious native seed grasses, and local fish that the men of the village expertly caught. The women we saw as patients almost invariably came to the clinics because their one- or two-year-old infants were showing signs of malnourishment. This was due largely to a widespread practice of prolonged breastfeeding, which was thought to prevent pregnancy. Unfortunately, this practice did not achieve the desired result, but did have the unintended effect of nutritionally starving young children, at a critical point in their development. So our efforts were mainly educational, though we also supplemented the diets of those children suffering from malnutrition.

After three or four months in Soroti, we were moved once more, this time to a camp near Entebbe on the northern shore of Lake Victoria. One of the largest fresh-water lakes in the world, this very impressive body of water was home to many beautiful species of birds. I spent a great deal of time walking beside this lake, enjoying the magnificent sight of white egrets, gannets, and eagles. There were many crocodiles, too, and I often found them sleeping on the riverbank in the midday heat. I was warned by others in the camp about the ferocity and speed of these creatures, and so avoided placing myself between a crocodile and its path of retreat to the river.

The atmosphere of the Entebbe camp was quite different from my two previous internments. Along with the single men, there were a few families and, soon after our arrival, an influx of both women and men from Baghdad. The new internees included a dozen or so women who were members of "the oldest profession," though their arrest by the British was not at all moralistic—merely the result of their status as foreigners. Among the Iraqis was an elderly pharmacist who was later indispensable to me, assisting in the camp's pharmacy, outpatient clinic, and hospital. As in Haifa and Soroti, I quickly volunteered my medical services, and after beginning with diagnostic lab studies, soon became involved in patient care. Some time later, I was immensely gratified by a medical promotion: I officially became the camp's medical officer. Now it was my responsibility to run our small hospital, located on a low hill overlooking the fenced camp compound, assisted in this work by a British medical matron from Entebbe. My other medical duties included managing the camp's clinic and pharmacy, as

During my internment in the Entebbe, Uganda, I was named
medical officer for the entire camp. This was my first real job as a
doctor, though I had yet to receive my medical degree. I am
standing in the back row, third from the left.

well as attending patients in a much larger hospital nearby. It was filled
with Italian prisoners of war who were brought to Entebbe after the 1935-
1936 conflict between Ethiopia and Mussolini's fascist Italy. In this facet
of my work I took a supporting role, and assisted the Italian physicians
who were interned along with their comrades.

Not only were circumstances for the practice of medicine in the Entebbe
camp a vast improvement over the previous camps, my duties as medical
officer were further supported by the world-famous British Yellow Fever
Institute, located just a short distance away. In my official role, I was entitled
to discuss problems with colleagues on staff there, and make use of their
well-stocked investigative laboratories. I also visited the Institute's library,
where I might supplement those few medical books still in my possession, and
begin studying for my final medical exams once more.

Life in the Entebbe camp was not *all* work and study, however—central
though these two pursuits were, and would remain. Among the Iraqi
internees was a young Romanian woman, tall and dark-haired, whose
name, I learned when introducing myself at dinner, was Daniela. Unlike
some among her compatriot internees, she was a good and solid person,
both sensitive and healthy. In time, we shared a cottage near the small
hilltop hospital where my duties as camp physician were based. Daniela

became involved in medicine, too, taking on strenuous duties as a nurse (of course, I could not help but notice how pretty she looked in her crisp uniform).

To relax, we took frequent walks together along the shoreline of Lake Victoria. Almost always deserted, I remember the lake as glistening and placid, the air as warm and still. This was an Africa that seemed to welcome us into the grandeur and drama of life. As I stood on the shore of this vast body of water, watching the white-plumed egrets catch fish and lift into the blue sky, the war and all its horrors seemed very far away. I might partially forget everything that happened in the previous years. And this brief respite from long-standing anxieties gladdened me, even awakening the impulse to practice the Catholic ritual of prayer that I learned in Malta. In prayer, I hoped to deepen this precious feeling of peace so I might hold onto it.

But there was something else in the Entebbe camp that temporarily relieved the oppression of our unrelenting uncertainty. The grounds boasted a largely British pastime, a quite good tennis court, where we played vigorously whenever we could. I remember playing several hard-fought sets of tennis, one afternoon, before finally sitting down to watch others volleying back and forth in the warm sunlight. All at once, I felt very cold and even began to shiver. It was several minutes before it dawned on me that I was exhibiting the symptoms of an illness for which I treated so many of my patients. After rushing to the laboratory, I put a drop of my blood on a microscope slide to study it, and was not at all surprised to see those

The microscope with which I repeatedly diagnosed my patients and myself with malaria and other tropical illnesses—throughout my tenure as the medical officer at a British internment camp near Entebbe, Uganda—during the latter part of the war.

familiar malarial parasites swarming within my red blood cells. I took a shot of quinine and a few atebrine tablets to cut the attack of malaria short, and recovered fully within several days' time.

When I'd been working in this camp for a good year, another of those truly magical moments occurred. On one of my regular trips to the city of Entebbe, to gather medicines and other supplies for our camp pharmacy, I noticed a large drum of petroleum jelly. Confiscated from the Italians, it sat behind some boxes in a corner of the British medical supply buildings. I inquired whether I might take this drum back to the camp, and since no one objected, carted it away.

Somehow, I had the presence of mind to realize I might turn this oily, creamy substance into cosmetics for women, every variety of which were quite scarce during the war years. My Iraqi pharmacist joined me in this enterprise, and we started a homegrown cosmetics manufacturing business. We also managed to secure a supply of yellow beeswax, since certain cosmetics required the stiffer consistency that this substance afforded. But we needed a more appealing base color, so we set the beeswax out to bleach in the sun, carefully positioning it on several flat rocks. In the space of a few days, it became a more useful waxy white color.

Consulting a pharmacological encyclopedia, we concocted formulas for face creams, astringent lotions, vanishing creams—even lipsticks, in the colors of cerise and carmine. Each day, we devoted many hours to mixing up batches of our line of simple but quite adequate cosmetics, and later packaged them in improvised containers.

Our lipstick packaging was our proudest invention. First, we poured the liquefied concoction into a glass test tube, where it cooled and hardened into a cylindrical shape. Then we knocked it from its glass mold and wrapped the brightly colored tube neatly in tin foil. Our final task was persuading the camp commandant to sell our wares. This he readily agreed to do, distributing our cosmetics to stores throughout the cities and towns of Uganda. In a month or so, after he collected the money from our cosmetics sales, he split the proceeds with us on a percentage basis. This transaction happened again and again over two years' time, and my share of our profits grew to several thousand English pounds—about fifteen thousand dollars—which, in those days, was a vast sum. I sorely needed this income to return to Malta and earn my degree. Like everyone else in our camp, I was virtually penniless, even though I labored seven days a week and, in any given month, cared for several dozen patients.

On the day we learned that World War II was finally over, I was officially interned in African camps for three and a half years. The unutterable devastation of this war was now at an end, Hitler was thoroughly defeated, and my passport was no longer a death sentence. I might return to my native country without fear. My thoughts were not, however, about returning to Austria. They were all about finishing my medical degree. I very much wanted to begin the full and legitimate practice of the profession I was occupied within for so long—prematurely performing a physician's role because of the war and its privations.

Not long after learning about our imminent release, my close companion, Daniela, prepared to return to her native Romania. In the days before her departure, we tried to adjust to our impending separation. Many nighttime hours were spent expressing our mutual gratitude for the solace we'd shared, while comforting each other that our intimacy was sadly at an end. When the day of her leave-taking arrived, we said our goodbyes with dignity. I then set off on a solitary walk, taking our usual route beside Lake Victoria. After several miles, I concluded that our being together had, in many ways, resembled a marriage. Several miles more, and it seemed an invaluable education I was very glad to have, particularly under these wartime circumstances.

Within a month, I was informed that my return trip to Malta was planned and paid for. The British kept their word, fully honoring my "right of return" to the place where they first interned me. This was a great relief. After all I'd been through, their diplomatic and generous travel arrangements seemed to represent the very best of what was meant by that familiar phrase, "the English character." On the morning of my departure, I lifted my two leather bags—those old friends who came with me from Graz—into the trunk of a car driving me to Kampala. Inside the interior pocket of one bag was my cosmetics fortune, my only means of securing my medical degree, once back in Malta. This neat stack of colorful English pounds was wrapped in paper, and concealed in a soft cloth bag that I found somewhere in my travels.

Now I was eager, even impatient, to set off. Though when I was at last settled in the car's back seat, being driven by a pleasant but taciturn British officer, I began to feel an unexpected melancholy. As the Ugandan countryside sped by, I realized the Entebbe camp was the scene of my first real experience of what it meant to be a physician: being counted-on for a diagnosis of what was medically wrong, and treating it successfully. I knew what the demands and rigors of medicine were like, now, for I'd seen them through, shouldering them again and again, day after day. I had also conducted—on that same, all-important, daily basis—my first real relationship with a woman.

After we traveled some distance, it came to me that the displacements of war quite inadvertently afforded me experiences more shattering to my worldview, more profoundly disturbing, than I might have in another time. I was not the same young man who said goodbye to his family and fiancée, seven years ago. My former life was torn apart during those years. My father killed. My mother repatriated to Yugoslavia. My brother settled in Palestine. And my fiancée gone. I'd heard nothing, nothing in several years, from Lizzie Biró. A decade or more later, I learned that Lizzie married during the war. Far more painfully, I also learned that she and her husband and family were probably sent, along with half a million other Hungarian Jews, to Nazi concentration camps in Poland, just as the war was ending. Hitler was desperate to exterminate as many European Jews as he could, before the complete collapse of his power. Lizzie and her family were most likely killed in a gas chamber, soon after their arrival in a camp, and turned to dust in a crematorium.

But as I rode to Kampala in 1945, none of this was known to me, and that ignorance was perhaps another of those circumstances that I can only think of as unusually fortuitous, if not magical. For though I now faced a much brighter future, I still had many emotional scars resulting from the war. And I have since learned that what strengthens us may also damage the well-knit fabric of our psyche, in ways that can be hidden from us. We need an interlude in which to heal, or at least "heal over," if we are to continue on with our lives in a reasonably productive way.

Watching the sky grow overcast while being driven away from the Entebbe camp, I grew increasingly sleepy and gradually dozed off. I do not know how long I slept, but when I woke suddenly from a dream, it was in a sweat of anxiety and fear. I dreamt that Lizzie and I were walking along the shoreline of a lake, when she quickly removed her arm from my arm, ran to the edge of the water, and dove in. *Crocodiles!* I bellowed after her. She surfaced, turned back and waved, then dove again beneath the waves. I ran along the shore trying to find her. After what seemed like hours, there was simply no sign. My despair that I was not able to save her was, in that moment of waking, very sharp and acute. *It was only a dream*, I told myself. *Only a dream.* But a feeling of terrifying helplessness remained with me during the entire drive to Kampala.

Several hours later, the British officer who was my driver stopped our car at the entrance of a hotel, not far from the bus station in Kampala. He unloaded my bags and handed me several pages of itinerary, as well as a thick envelope of tickets. I would board a bus the next day for Pakwach, he told me. This was a small town north of Lake Albert, the lake from which the White Nile flowed. I'd then travel north along the Nile by boat to Laropi, and continue on from there for over a thousand river miles, eventually reaching the port of Alexandria. From there, I would take a ship back to Malta. Like all my other accommodations on this return trip, my reservation at the Kampala hotel was already paid for, so my only concern was arriving on time for the bus the next morning.

A few minutes later, I was taken to my hotel room. When I saw the smooth chenille bedspread, the polished wood of the night table, the bathroom displaying an assortment of clean towels, these items immediately reminded me of so many other hotel rooms I'd stayed in. Though this was the first time I enjoyed such familiar, impersonal comfort in many years.

As I lay in bed that night, preparing for sleep at an early hour, to be rested for the long journey ahead, I thought of the way our lives were lived within a matrix of ties to other people—even though all our ties inevitably dissolved. Though not completely: our connections eventually "distilled," or were reduced to a form that no longer felt quite so vital or alive. But a tie integral to our essential being did not distill, it seemed to me. Instead, our integral ties disappeared whole, sinking beneath the urgency and clamor of each lived day, buried beneath the daily tumult.

As I turned these and other thoughts over and over in my mind, I drifted off, and did not wake until the next morning, when I sprang out of bed to look at my watch. It was then I realized that, overnight, I somehow readied myself for my return to Malta.

After taking breakfast in the hotel, my long bus trip to Pakwach in northern Uganda was tiring yet uneventful. Though I did see far more of the African countryside than I'd seen during all the years I lived on this vast and varied continent. Villages of thatched and rounded huts resembling upside-down birds' nests passed by, as did glimpses of men and boys in tribal dress. A minimum of clothing, or none at all, seemed a wise adaptation to equatorial life, with its perpetually hot weather. As I listened to the incessant, thrumming whine of the bus motor, I found myself daydreaming, mentally revisiting the places in Malta I'd known so well: the University and the hospital wards, my small flat, the Gegg's house, *Actione Catholica*, the Cathedral of St. John. Had they withstood the heavy German bombing reported in the newspapers?

Fourteen thousands bombs were dropped on the Maltese archipelago, even though those small, rocky islands together comprised a mere hundred and twenty-two square miles. During one brutal, six-month period, Malta withstood five separate attacks by over one hundred Stuka dive-bombers and Messerschmitt fighters, on a daily basis. The islands were key to controlling the sea lanes supplying the forces of both sides, so they were fought over with unrelenting ferocity. I'd read that Malta was bombed more times during the war than any other place on Earth. Ultimately, of course, the British and Allied troops prevailed, but given that pulverizing, two-year onslaught, what might I hope to find upon my return?

As if on cue, the people I'd known on Malta appeared briefly in my mind's eye. Father Laspina and the joyfully comic sight of him playing soccer with his priestly black robes hitched-up. Tom Shockledge swimming in the sea off Sliema. Mr. Pace and his bushy eyebrows, his kind expression. The many other students I'd known at the university. The three members of the Gegg family. James Mercieca and his father, the Chief Justice of Malta. Herr Mueller, who'd marked my passport with a "J." I imagined the British would return the Geggs, the Merciecas, and Herr Mueller to Malta, too, though I'd heard nothing of their circumstances since the beginning of our internment in different camps. But these fleeting images of my Maltese friends soon gave way to strange dreams, as my bus traveled all through the night. We arrived in Pakwach, a small town above Lake Albert, around noon the next day. I'd not slept well, but was glad to complete the first real leg of my journey, and soon set off carrying my bags toward the docks on the Nile River. Asking around, I located my boat, handed over my ticket, and was shown a quite small cubicle of a room containing a single bed. Stacking my bags against one wall, I stretched out, intending to rest briefly, before looking around the boat. When I woke several hours later, it was late afternoon. I could tell by the vibrations that rose through the floorboards that the boat was moving. I sighed, then turned over and pulled a blanket around my shoulders. I thought about getting up and finding some dinner, but the decision was made for me: I quickly fell asleep once more.

The next morning, voices nearby—combining in a kind of counterpoint with far away shouts—woke me abruptly. I got up, washed and shaved quickly, then went out onto the deck. The river glittered softly in the early morning sun, and the boat was peopled by deck hands and a smattering of passengers. We were headed for Laropi, now just three hundred kilometers away. Within a few hours, I knew my way around, had eaten breakfast, and carried a heavy medical textbook over to a vacant chair on the far side of the deck. I intended to study as I watched the shoreline go by. Opening my book, I braced one foot against a gray pipe, the lower of two parallel ship railings. After reading a few paragraphs, I was again daydreaming of Malta, this time about completing my studies after years away from medical school. How would I adjust to classrooms and exam-taking, after years of performing as a doctor, and being thought of as such? I had another year of course work, in concert with the usual hospital rotations, but I knew my time in Africa greatly matured my medical understanding and skills. Then it seemed as if my former competitiveness began to stir from its long dormancy, as I imagined testing my new skills in the laboratory of an educational environment. But I soon dismissed this fantasy as ridiculous, even unseemly. And that led to the realization that I had grown into adulthood, in some indefinable way. But this was to be expected, I told myself: in April, I turned thirty.

Looking up from my book and my daydreams, I gazed across the water and studied the shoreline. A pile of logs appeared near the water's edge. When one log moved its branches, I realized I was looking at a group of crocodiles soaking up warmth in the late afternoon sun. I looked back down at my book, intending to concentrate on my reading, but an unwanted image from that terrible dream of Lizzie diving into crocodile-infested waters came back to me. And with it, a wave of guilt and remorse. In fact, I suddenly felt quite ill. Leaping up, I rushed to the lavatory. Somehow, despite all my precautions, I managed to get dysentery again, something I and many others were plagued by in the internment camps. This new onslaught of amoebic parasites must have contributed to my recent tiredness. So as not to suffer dehydration, I filled a canteen with water and took it with me to my sleeping cubicle. There I added two water purifying tablets before drinking my fill. Lying down to read, I spent the remainder of that day reading and making quick lavatory trips, while taking some medication I carried with me from Entebbe. By next morning, my symptoms abated. I took up my station on deck, reading several dense chapters in my medical text, and pausing, from time to time, to think about my family. Though I at some point learned that my mother re-married (her second husband was a man from Budapest whose Protestantism kept her safe during the war), I'd not heard from Elserl or my brother, in some time. I wondered what the end of the war meant in their lives. That night, I was able to stay on deck and gaze at the stars, identifying several that Herr Schmidt taught me the names of in the Haifa camp, which now seemed a lifetime ago. I also enjoyed the night sounds, which seemed a lush orchestration: there were thousands of calls and strange trills, punctuated by the splashes of fish diving ahead of the ship's bow. So many of Africa's creatures were nocturnal, and the night was teeming with life.

After we docked in Laropi a day later, I was transferred to a sturdy, dust-covered truck for the next leg of my journey. As we climbed the foothills dividing Uganda from Sudan, the roads were quite rutted, and the truck was both old and noisy. So the ambient sound that accompanied our forward progress drowned out all but my most immediate thoughts. Traveling the whole day, we arrived in Juba before nightfall. I located my hotel and, after a good long bath and a night's rest in a bed that was not rocked by either waves or rutted roads, I set off to find the boat that would carry me for nearly two thousand kilometers along the Nile River to Khartoum.

As it turned out, this ship was twice the size of the previous one. My cabin on the Isis' upper deck was luxurious by comparison, and the dining room was resplendent with tablecloths and full place settings. A surprising sigh of relief rose from the center of my being. The new ship's amenities pleased my sensibilities and reassured me. Though I knew it was simply the upcoming depth of the river that made passage for this larger, more comfortable vessel possible, I nevertheless felt that the journey to Khartoum, which covered less than a third of the Nile's over four thousand miles, was quite long enough.

As I stood on deck that afternoon, watching the riverbanks flow by at a greater distance than before, I tried to remember what I'd learned in the *Realgymnasium* about the history of the Nile. I recalled how it seemed a mythical place and not quite real, perhaps because I was only then familiar with my own country, in addition to Hungary and Italy. Though I still recalled that phrase, "the cradle of civilization," referring to the Nile River as the first place on Earth that human culture flourished. But this fact was known to us only because hieroglyphic records were preserved in the Egyptian pyramids.

By contrast, the war seemed to me an effort to destroy the civilizing impulse, particularly as witnessed by the chilling spectacle of book burning in the Nazi Germany of 1933. It was Heinrich Heine, the great German poet my father loved to read, who prophetically wrote, "Where books are burned, in the end people too are burned." These thoughts of course led me to remember the letter from Elserl about Father. I usually tried to avoid this memory, having learned that dwelling upon my inability to save him would lead me to despair. And then, my despair would turn to anger that had no productive avenue of expression. But my ties to my family were, I realized, my essential ties, and they were buried whole beneath the immediate demands of my daily life. This seemed true, of course, for everyone: we all hold our essential human ties close to our heart.

The Isis passed several small towns in succession—Tambe, Shambe, Tonga—and was headed toward Malakal before continuing on to Kaka and Ar Rank. Though larger, this ship was not fast. My trip to Khartoum was scheduled to take the better part of two weeks. In that time, I learned the deck hands and other Egyptian workers were friendly if addressed directly, but talked chiefly among themselves. One early evening, though, I looked up from reading to see many odd shapes bobbing in the river. They were just far enough away that I was unable to see what they were. When I asked a deckhand, he laughed a short, lilting laugh and called out to another man in Arabic. This man called back one word, which he pronounced with an emphasis on the first syllable.

"EE-pot-mous! EE-pot-mous!"

"Hippo-pot-a-mus!" I called out in reply, understanding what the bobbing shapes were when his approximated English name gave me a clue.

"Is it! Is it!" this man enthusiastically called back.

Meanwhile, the hippos reached shore and waddled up onto land. I'd never seen such large, fat and odd-looking creatures. They looked strangely pregnant, and I was put in mind of that other phrase, "the fertile Nile River valley." I watched them for as long as they were visible, their movements fascinating to me, a European unused to this sort of wildlife.

Continuing on our long journey, we docked at many of the small towns we passed, but our stops were fairly brief, with not enough time to go ashore and explore the countryside. In this stop-and-start manner, we moved along the Nile, passing the last three towns on our itinerary—Al Jabalyn, Kusti, and Al Qutaynah—before arriving in Khartoum, the place where the White Nile joins the Blue Nile (so named for the characteristic color of the water).

Disembarking in Khartoum, I was gratified to be on stationary ground and do such ordinary things as order a meal in a restaurant, or sit at a small table outside a coffeehouse. But here—unlike that memorable day in Trieste, when I drank espresso with my fellow Austrians—I was totally alone. Having just purchased cigarettes, I was opening the pack when something about this simple and habitual act caused me to remember a look Daniela used to give me. And I was soon confronting a loneliness that I'd not felt in a long time, pushing back the pressure of tears gathering behind my eyes. By now, Daniela would have begun her life in Romania again. I knew she would be just fine, as she was an intelligent, resourceful kind of person. A sigh escaped from deep within my being. What a circuitous route my life had taken—since the day I put my ticket to an unknown place named Malta inside the wallet my mother gave me. And I was now sailing to Malta, once again.

My thoughts turned to that magical good fortune which came to my rescue, again and again, and helped me to circumvent the obstacles I faced. There were times when, I must admit, it was difficult to look my good fortune in the eye—aware, as I was, of the many people whose luck had lapsed, both before and during the war. In this regard, I thought often of Lizzie, and my aunts and uncles, hoping for their safety. The only way I could justify, or even live with, my good fortune, was to believe there was something I was meant to accomplish, something for the sake of which I was helped to survive and continue on with my life.

After a few days in Khartoum, I boarded another boat, this one headed for the city of Aswan in southeastern Egypt. From there, I took a train to Cairo, where I spent a week in an elegant old Hilton Hotel. Just hours after making myself at home in my new room, with its view of a city-square park, my earlier episodes of malaria and dysentery both relapsed. I spent a good deal of time tending to these ailments. But when, after a few days, I was for the most part recovered, I walked to a store specializing in international goods and bought a few European newspapers. I was eager to know what was occurring in the world during the aftermath of the war. London was in the midst of rubble-clearing, planning to rebuild landmarks and other buildings, destroyed by air attacks during the Blitz. Clearing and rebuilding was the common theme in reports from other European countries, as well, but I was disappointed that there was no specific news about Graz.

Taking more ambitious walks around Cairo a day later, it surprised me to encounter small groups of English and French tourists. Though I was pleased to see them, since it meant the world was returning to a state of normalcy. In the spirit of a normalizing, post-war tourism, I decided to take a bus about fifteen miles west of Cairo. Near the village of Abu Rawash, there was a pyramid whose central chamber was exposed by damage that was inflicted by the Romans, many centuries earlier. The bus ride might afford a view of the land surrounding the city, something I was keen to see.

But the trip was forgettable. Only the nearly five-thousand-year-old ruins were worth seeing. The main pyramid at this excavation site was built by the third pharaoh to rule during Egypt's Fourth Dynasty, and was romantically named "Djedefre's Starry Sky." I thought immediately of the irony of this name, given that stars were now visible from the open burial chamber. The overall atmosphere was, in fact, similar to something bombed: rubble, rocks, and mounds of dirt were everywhere. But there was still a mysterious and unusual presence about the place. Especially if, after gazing at those massive, crumbling blocks of stone, one walked down steep stairs leading into the below-ground central chamber. Standing silently in the center of this room, I could feel the wind of ancient times whistling softly past.

My remaining days in Cairo were not eventful, though I did enjoy gazing at the city's beautiful rose and white stone buildings as I walked around the marketplace. By the time I boarded a train for the main Egyptian port of Alexandria, on the Mediterranean coast, I was prepared to say a fond silent farewell to the continent of Africa. From Alexandria, I'd take the final trip of my three-thousand-mile journey from Entebbe, and sail back to the island of Malta. Upon my return, I hoped to resume my medical studies at the Royal University, once more.

∞

CHAPTER FIVE

Valletta, Malta
London, England
Winter, 1945 ~ Fall, 1948

When my ship from Alexandria sailed into the Grand Harbor at Valletta, it was a brilliant sunlit morning. As we drew nearer to the docks, I felt embraced by the sun-washed, limestone cliffs, rising steeply from the blue and sparkling sea. Five long years had passed since I'd been here last, and as I studied the harbor's encircling, cream-colored stone, I experienced a flash of visceral remembering. For a few seconds, I felt the presence of the younger man I'd once been, before my forced departure from Malta. Both dismayed by the difference and oddly gratified, I realized that my understanding of the world had clarified and deepened since then. And it seemed to me that a partially concealed fruit of my internment years was a form of wisdom that only experience could provide.

Hoisting my heavy suitcases, I walked away from the docks and continued up the hill toward the center of town. I was surprised by all the cars and people filling the streets, and realized I expected to find a much quieter place in the wake of the war. But like the inhabitants of Malta, perhaps, I now felt far more prepared for whatever might come my way. I'd proven myself to myself, and knew my skills were sufficient to survive in the world.

Not only that, but what I had to offer was, I slowly realized, much needed. I'd found a reason for being—one that, in reaching over the little concerns of self-interest, sustained me through my dedication to its unfolding. In other words, it gave me what I gave it, in like measure, and in this way formed an enclosing circle, a harbor's embrace.

Reaching Valletta's main street, I could plainly see the destruction inflicted by hundreds of German bombers. Some time later, I read several newspaper accounts about life on Malta during the war. Thirty thousand buildings were turned to rubble, while an entire population, with barely enough food to survive, were afraid for their lives, for years on end. When the war was finally over, the casualties on Malta were officially listed at fifteen hundred, an enormous number for a country so small.

Yet on this sunlit morning, the people crowding the streets seemed undeterred by the aftermath of war. They were busily engaged in living their lives. No one could bring back what was gone, their activity seemed to suggest, and the only real choice was to carry on.

Before too long, thankfully, as my suitcases seemed to grow more burdensome by the minute, I found an inexpensive hotel not far from the Royal University. Economy was a necessity, as my expenses were now wholly my own responsibility, and my toiletries fortune needed to last until I secured a job as a practicing physician. And so, before leaving my room at the hotel, I searched for a place to conceal my precious stack of British pounds. A careful study of the room's furnishings revealed a wobbly bureau drawer that might serve my purpose well. I removed the drawer, wedged my money against the bureau's rear panel, and slid the drawer back into place. It shut against the carved front panel in a loose way, and looked nearly the same as before. Satisfied, I changed my jacket and set out to find my friend, Father Laspina.

As I approached the Cathedral of St. John, it seemed miraculously undamaged. Closer still, I saw that it escaped all harm during the devastating wartime bombing. Once inside the cathedral's immense double doors, I was greeted by hundreds of votive candles flickering on the distant altar. The glow of candlelight was lovely, and reflected in thousands of gilt-inlaid frescoes, glittering across the entire expanse of the vast arched ceiling. I remembered gazing at the cathedral's astoundingly rich Baroque art during my first stay on Malta. But as I stood there once more, quietly absorbing the atmosphere of this place, I tried to breathe in its immensity and stillness, the profundity of its peace. I wanted to walk down an aisle and find a solitary pew to sit and pray, but felt anxious to find Father Laspina.

"You've come back!" he exclaimed, with a broad smile and a warm gleam in his eyes, as I entered his office at *Actione Catholica*.

"Yes, and I wanted to see you before I did anything else. I'm so glad you've come through in fine shape!"

He shook my hand and we embraced. Then we talked about my years in Haifa and Africa, and he told me about his work here during the war. Despite the fact that many hours each day were necessarily spent in underground bomb shelters, he tried to help the young people, women, and children who remained—the only Maltese not drafted for the war effort. As we talked, I realized that we both felt much older than before the war years, even though Father Laspina was then barely forty, and I just turned thirty in the spring.

As I was about to take my leave, being equally eager to discuss my future with Mr. Pace at the university, and hoping he too had survived the war, we shook hands and Father Laspina said, "It is *good* to see you, Hans. We must have dinner together soon, and talk more." I felt elated that my old friend was still a benevolent presence in my life. The warmth of our friendship made me feel a little less alone in the world.

Entering the building that housed the Royal University's administrative offices, I located Mr. Pace's secretary and asked if I might have a word with him. She went to inquire. In a few minutes, Mr. Pace welcomed me into his office and I sat in a chair positioned in front of his broad and ancient desk. He was still, I noticed gratefully, the same kind and understanding older man I'd known before. We talked in a circumspect way about where I'd been and what I'd done, how I'd studied diligently all the while, and was now very eager to complete my degree. Mr. Pace asked his secretary to locate my old records. Scanning them briefly, he outlined a year-long course of study, hospital rounds, and final exams intended to culminate in my medical degree. As we shook hands, I felt immensely relieved that the final phase of my long journey toward becoming a doctor was finally arranged, and scheduled to commence within the week.

But not all of my reunions on Malta were happy ones. During the first week after my return, I learned that my good friend, Tom Shockledge, did not survive the war. A few days later, I went to visit his mother. She needed a sympathetic listener, and was soon telling me the story of what happened to her son. Tom was a medical officer in the British army, she told me, and while stationed at a hospital in Palestine, was killed by the Jewish terrorist group known as the *Irgun*. Years later, I learned that the

British were then refusing entry into Palestine to boatloads of Jewish refugees stranded off the coast. The *Irgun's* terrorist activity was, at that point, in protest against restrictive British immigration policies, as well as their ruling presence—a presence mandated twenty-five years earlier by the League of Nations.

I told Mrs. Shockledge how much Tom's friendship meant to me when I was a stranger in strange country. I described our camaraderie in the hospital and at university, as well as our afternoons spent swimming at the rocky beach in Sliema. She and I wept together in our mutual grief over her son's murder, and she thanked me again and again for sharing my memories of Tom. As I walked slowly back to my hotel room, I was touched by her gratitude, despite such inconsolable grief. It was terribly sad for her to lose the son of whom she was so very proud.

There were so many losses on Malta. Even the famous Maltese falcons were now gone, those peregrine falcons whose association with the islands began, I read, in the sixteenth century. Nearly four hundred years before, the king of Spain bestowed Malta upon the Knights of St. John, in return for a "tax" of one trained hunting falcon, presented on the first day of November each year. But after the war, the birds never returned. Their habitat, one of the best for falcons in all of Europe, was violently disturbed by the bombing.

My friends, the Geggs, did not come back, either. Herr Gegg wrote several times about his family's decision to return to Germany after the war, because they now felt unwelcome on Malta. But the fates of several others remained a mystery. James Mercieca and his father, the Chief Justice, along with Herr Mueller, were all missing. I wondered if they, too, found safe haven in another country.

The year very quickly ended and, just as quickly, 1946 began, during which I completed my final studies and hospital rotations, and took my written, oral, and practicum exams. These tripartite exams tested my knowledge of internal medicine and surgery, obstetrics and gynecology, pediatrics, otolaryngology, infectious diseases, and dermatology. Some exams I sat for with members of the current final year class, and some I completed separately. But after my long years of study and practical experience, I passed each one easily, as if jumping over a series of not-too-high hurdles. Then I waited for over a week—somewhat impatiently, I must admit—before receiving notification of my graduation date.

Since I'd finished my studies and taken my exams on a different timetable than any other student, and because the war delayed the completion of my formal training so excessively long, administrators at the Royal University decided to present my degree during a ceremony planned for me alone. I entered the university under unusual circumstances, and I was leaving it in the same manner.

In January of 1947, on a sunny Monday afternoon, I sat in the academic assembly hall, dressed in my doctoral robe and wearing a *barretta*, a ceremonial, crown-like cap similar to the hats worn by Catholic bishops.

A formal graduation portrait taken on Malta in 1947.
I am wearing my doctoral robe and barretta cap,
while holding my medical degree, at long last.

Nervously, as if I were about to give a piano recital, I watched Mr. Gouci, the University Rector, and Mr. Pace, the University Secretary, as well as the Bishop of Malta and Father Laspina take their positions on the stage. One by one, they stood at the podium and gave a brief speech about my unusual academic career, while wishing me a bright future as a newly degreed physician. Then it was my turn to rise, walk up the side stairs, and make my way self-consciously to the middle of the stage. Standing before a large audience of university friends and acquaintances, I accepted my rolled parchment diploma, the achievement for which I waited so long and labored under so many circumstances. It was a brief but very moving moment in time. A hush seemed to fall over those gathered in the assembly hall, lasting until after I returned to my seat.

During the reception held immediately afterwards, I accepted warm congratulations from professors, fellow students, acquaintances, and friends. Later on, before this memorable and long-awaited day was over, a photographer took several graduation pictures to commemorate the occasion. In one of these, I am wearing my robe and holding my rolled-up diploma, while Father Laspina stands like a guardian angel behind me.

Another graduation photograph taken on Malta,
this one with my good friend and "guardian angel,"
Father Laspina, standing beside me.

Since no one in my family could attend, there was no one to give me the traditional graduation present. But Father Laspina surprised my expectations by presenting me with something I lacked for a very long time: a handsome leather briefcase. It was quite like him to be this thoughtful and generous on my behalf, and his kind act reminded me that I often thought of Father Laspina (along with certain members of the university faculty and administration) as part of my Maltese family. I was then young enough to find this substitute for my own family an essential experience, and it truly sustained me in my long exile from Austria.

When I returned to my room that night, I unrolled my new diploma and studied every detail: the thickness of the paper, the Gothic script, the names, the dates, and the inked signatures. Nothing escaped my rapt attention. I was hardly able to believe that I my doctorate was finally in my possession. Before going to bed, I fitted my diploma into my new briefcase for safe-keeping, and then—knowing it was a bit silly, but unable to stop myself—I put the briefcase under the pillow next to mine on my double bed. If I woke up in the night, I could easily reach out to make sure it was still there.

Several days later, on the day I left Malta for the last time, I woke to the unmistakable sound of a steady rainfall. Despite the weather, Father Laspina came to see me off. He stood on the dock under the sheltering dome of a coal-black umbrella, dripping with rain. And before I walked up the ramp to the ship's deck, he gave me his blessing. I thanked him once more for all he'd done for me. "I will be sure to write," I said, feeling that I did not want to lose our close connection. It seemed too sudden and final a break with this compassionate man, whose calmly vital presence was so important to me—to my very survival. As my ship pulled away from the dock, I watched Father Laspina wave a last time and, as the rain was now a drenching downpour, walk quickly up the hill.

Looking out toward the open sea, it seemed Malta's Grand Harbor opened her sheltering arms wide to let me go. I was blessed, and now I was being released into the wide world to encounter the unknown once more. This was of course exciting. But it was also unsettling for someone whose life was uprooted again and again during the previous decade, and whose responses from time to time revealed small signs of the injury these many uprootings caused. In today's terms, it was called "post-traumatic stress syndrome." But in the forties it was known, if it was known at all, by the far more generalized term of "shell-shock."

As a result, my steamer passage across the Mediterranean to Marseilles was spent in a fog of contradictory emotions. I felt hopeful and optimistic, one minute, and quite lost and alone, the next. From now on, I anxiously realized, no one knew who I was. My mother and brother, my aunts, uncles, cousins, grandmother, and fiancée, Lizzie, all seemed very far away—as if they were part of another life, entirely. I held them in my heart, but a supportive social fabric was not only missing, it seemed likely to elude me for quite some time to come.

Perhaps this was another reason why Father Laspina was so vitally important. He helped me, a foreigner whose former life and family were far away, to feel as if I mattered to other people. It seemed odd that this experience, so easily taken for granted, was so essential to one's well-being— the experience of being seen, acknowledged, and known. And so, I thought, *How precious these invisible gifts we unknowingly give each other are.*

The evening my ship reached Marseilles, I disembarked and found a hotel for the night, intending to take a train to the north of France and the English Channel port of Calais, the next morning. For years, I was moved from internment camp to internment camp, after which I returned to my former life as a medical student. But in all that time, I never experienced an interlude like this one, in which I existed without a larger context, a role. Being deprived of all human connections, even ones enforced from outside, was difficult and even disturbing. It's true there was my career in medicine to guide and shape my energies and my days. But before I was able to turn my attention to my career, there was this present period of free-fall, in which I had no place of belonging and no semblance of a home.

The next day, I used my slightly rusty but still adequate French to order breakfast in a café. Later on, I located the railway station, and there I waited several hours for an overnight train to Calais. After presenting my old Austrian passport to a train official, I sat beside a window. As towns flew past like a swiftly moving river, I felt dazed by my inner turmoil and tired from a sleep-disturbed night in a strange hotel room. From time to time, groups of buildings destroyed during the war came into view, now they were just piles of rubble left behind by the *Luftwaffe*. I'd read that the English were completely defeated in Calais, forced to retreat from this last of their remaining strongholds in France. They left behind a small group of men who were charged with holding this hopeless position, though they knew quite well it was about to be crushed by the German onslaught. As a result, I was prepared to see far worse destruction when we entered Calais, but there was no time to look around. The ferry boat to the port of Southampton in England was departing shortly, and I climbed aboard with my two suitcases and all-important briefcase, for the trip across the English Channel.

In Southampton, some hours later, I found my way to yet another train station and purchased a ticket to London. As I waited for my train's departure, conscious that this was my first time on English soil, I read the *London Times* and learned about government plans to fill the many bomb craters made by the Blitz. From the autumn of 1940 to the spring of 1941, England's major cities were bombarded with devastating incendiary and high explosive bombs by Hitler's forces. During one sustained attack lasting fifty-seven consecutive nights, a third of the city of London was destroyed. Not even Buckingham Palace, the London residence of King George VI and Queen Elizabeth, as well as their two daughters, the future Queen Elizabeth II and her sister, Princess Margaret, was spared during the Blitz.

When the call came to board, I again found a window seat, so I might see the English landscape. Hour after hour passed, as I listened to the soft clickety-clack of the train speeding along its tracks, while intermittently reading one of my medical books. It was evening by the time my train from Southampton pulled into Victoria Railway Station in London. I felt immediately overwhelmed by the absolute chaos of train station activity. Hundreds of people were rushing through, going home after work, while loudspeakers squawked, and the brakes and engines of arriving and departing trains alternately squealed and roared. Everyone seemed to know exactly where they were going, and I felt suddenly very diminished and forlorn. After sitting on a bench for a little while to adjust to it all, I decided to hail a cab and ask to be taken to a local hotel. Struggling inside the lobby with my luggage, I registered at the front desk and was then shown my room. After washing up and resting briefly, I walked downstairs and asked directions to a nearby restaurant. There I had an English dinner of boiled vegetables and equally well-boiled meat, with a custard-like dessert served with strong, dark tea. I walked back to my room in a more leisurely, exploring-the-city sort of way, and though I soon went tiredly to bed, I did manage to scan the classified section of the *Times*, looking for a rental room in a house outside of central London. To my relief, there were several good possibilities, and after talking with two or three prospective landlords the next day, I took a bus to Finsbury Park in north London to look at an advertised room.

The quite adequate room I was shown occupied the second floor of a medium-sized, pleasant home. Public transport was nearby, and there was a charming backyard greenhouse with a small garden beyond it, as well. The next day, I moved into this quiet house inhabited by the Wright family (a grandfather, grandmother, and granddaughter—a plump young woman who worked in a dentist's office, located on the ground floor of a house several blocks away).

Finsbury Park got its name from a nearby public park built during the Victorian Era. And residential housing soon grew up around this park, due to a burgeoning population of Londoners. On weekends, in spring and summer of that year, after I and everyone else endured one of the bitterest, snow-buried winters in London's history, I often walked through the park, homesick for my Austrian Alps. Finsbury Park was not at all alpine, of course, but the sight of trees, while being in the fresh outdoor air, was something I very much needed. To me, it was a kind of home.

Before I moved into Finsbury Park, however, I was forced to confront a new impasse. The General Medical Council of England was unable to accept my Maltese medical credentials, without proof of being permitted to practice in that country. I was dumbfounded by this new barrier to my professional life, and not knowing how to proceed, decided to visit the British Colonial Office, thinking they might be able to help.

Fortunately, the official with whom I discussed my situation was both sympathetic and effective. He sent a telegram to the Governor of Malta, asking for a written statement giving me permission to practice medicine in that country, from the date I received my degree until several weeks afterwards. This was a period of time long enough to satisfy the

General Medical Council, and my name was soon included in the official list of overseas physicians entitled to practice in the U.K. I was now able to look for work, and I soon applied for and was given an evening practice post in a private clinic in the north of London, not too far from Finsbury Park.

Every weeknight, from six in the evening until ten, I saw patients at the clinic and made house calls, attending those too ill to come in for an office visit. The income from my clinic work was sufficient to support my basic needs, and it supplemented my limited savings, what little remained from the Ugandan cosmetics trade.

Meanwhile, I made a point of learning about the residency programs then available in London, and decided to apply to the Great Ormond Street Hospital for Sick Children. I was convinced this was the best place to obtain my postgraduate training, as it afforded me the chance to earn a Diploma in Child Health and the residency was supplemented by lectures in pediatrics at the University of London. Great Ormond Street Hospital was a very well-regarded institution, and was famously bequeathed the copyright to *Peter Pan* by its author, J.M. Barrie. Over the years, income from this fanciful tale about a boy who never wanted to grow up, and whose best friend was a fairy named "Tinkerbell," funded all manner of medical programs for children.

After I was accepted for residency training, I soon discovered that the patient population at Great Ormond Street Hospital was a highly diverse one, since London welcomed waves of immigrants from India, Pakistan, the Caribbean, Africa, and other countries around the world, right after the war. There were many wards full of children, all of whom were gratifyingly able to respond to my treatment, and I tended both babies and pre-school children, visiting my patients seven days a week. My residency was a good refinement of my general medical training, and coming to know and care for so many children prepared me in some small way, I later felt, for fatherhood.

My clinic duties, on the other hand, involved patients of all ages. But my responsibilities at the clinic ended when the week ended. This left me with a bit of free time on weekends to begin dating a young woman I met in a bookstore near the University of London. Elise Nottingham was studying art history and dreaming of someday assisting a museum curator. As we both loved the fresh outdoor air, we soon fell into the habit of taking peripatetic weekend walking tours of London, after my rounds at the hospital were done. On many of these occasions, we found ourselves wandering the rooms of the National Gallery, on the north side of Trafalgar Square, not all that far from the University of London. One afternoon, I remember being struck by a small painting titled "St. Paul Shipwrecked on Malta." It was by Adam Elsheimer, a sixteenth century German Baroque painter who worked for Pope Paul V, as the accompanying plaque explained. St. Paul, the story went, was shipwrecked on Malta in 60 A.D., and was the first to bring Christianity to the Maltese. Impressed by his miraculous ability to heal the sick, they flocked to see him in large numbers during his three-month stay on the island. It occurred to me that Father Laspina was a spiritual descendant of St. Paul, for he too seemed to heal those who came to see him.

That same afternoon, as Elise and I were wandering through the National Gallery's vast collection, she entertained me, as she often did, by recounting the scholarly research and opinions of her art history teachers. One professor recently told Elise's class that, during the war, Hitler and the Nazi party took priceless works of art from private and public collections throughout Europe. What was worse, the whereabouts of thousands of pieces of this stolen art was completely unknown. Certainly, I found the subject intriguing, but the mention of Hitler's name was so abhorrent to me that I did little to encourage this conversational thread. We moved on to other subjects, walking slowly from room to room.

But when I returned to Finsbury Park that night, I felt very troubled. When Elise mentioned the name of that madman, a dark cloud appeared and I found myself worrying about my mother, my brother, and fiancée, Lizzie. Over the years, letters from Elserl and Pauli were few, often arriving years apart. We lost touch some time ago, and I'd not heard from my family in half a year. But a few weeks later, I learned that a friend of mine was planning to attend an industrial exhibition in Budapest, Hungary, along with others in his field of industrial engineering. Here was my chance.

I arranged to accompany the industrial exhibit group to Budapest, as fares were less expensive this way, and for the first time in ten years, I was able to see my mother again. She was overjoyed to see me, as I was to see her, though we had no real privacy while we talked. She was living in very crowded conditions, then a commonplace in Communist Hungary. The state owned and controlled nearly everything, enforcing various ill-fated programs that eventually devastated the post-war economy.

I also met Elserl's second husband, Gyorgy Hevesy, on that brief visit. He was a very nice man with the good fortune to be blond and blue-eyed, so he fit the Aryan "racial" ideal of Nazi ideology. This fact, along with his Protestantism, shielded my mother from the fate of many Hungarian Jews during the last years of the war. For by the time of my visit, Elserl learned

My mother, Elserl, with her second husband, Gyorgy Hevesy.
His blond, blue-eyed appearance protected my mother during the
remaining years of the war because the Nazis assumed that she,
like her husband, was not Jewish.

that Lizzie not only married during the years of our enforced separation, she and her husband were among those taken to the concentration camps to be murdered, just prior to the German surrender.

Hearing this horrific news for the first time, I felt as if punched in the stomach and it was hard to breathe. Elserl tried to comfort me—as I tried to comfort her about the loss of Father and our family life together—but I knew it would take a very long time for us to bury all our losses. There were only a few days to catch up, in any case, before I returned to London once more. But I spent many months thinking about Lizzie in every spare minute. I was unable to believe she was dead. She was young, attractive, lively. It was all too unbearably sad.

A month or two after my return from Budapest, my residency at the Great Ormond Street Hospital came to an end, and after passing the required examination, I received my Diploma in Child Health. In the interim, I learned that jobs for physicians were now difficult to find in London, or anywhere else in England. Doctors returning from military service needed all the available jobs, and were clearly given preference over an outsider like myself. Here was yet another impasse.

But, unlike all the previous impasses, this one was resolved easily. I simply applied for a position with the British Colonial Service and, not long afterward, heard of an interesting opening in Georgetown, British Guiana, on the northern coast of South America. The job provided for an initial, two-year term of service, followed by home leave in London, at which point a more permanent appointment was available. I accepted this post without hesitation when it was offered, and was told I'd sail for British Guiana within a week.

CHAPTER SIX

Georgetown, British Guiana
London, England
  Georgetown / London
Fall, 1948 ~ Spring, 1960

At the end of the first year of what later became many years of residence in England, I said my farewells to the elderly Wrights. But as I warmly thanked them for their kind hospitality, a sudden feeling of gratitude welled-up within me, one I struggled to conceal. I did not understand this unexpected depth of emotion, and didn't wish to reveal it in my confusion. But as I shook their soft worn hands, it occurred to me, for the first time, that the Wrights reminded me of my older relatives. Perhaps because they and their granddaughter, Cecilia, welcomed me into their pleasant and quiet family home.

It was a good place to study early in the morning, before leaving for my medical rounds at Great Ormond Street Hospital, lectures at the University of London, and evenings of patient care at the clinic. The many people I'd come to know in these medical and university settings figured importantly, too, and I made sure to thank each one while saying my goodbyes. In between, I spent my last hours with Elise Nottingham. We walked and talked as we'd done so many times before. Both of us knew that ours was not destined to be a lasting romance, but it was a good and worthy friendship, nonetheless.

In the years that followed, I came to understand the surprising emotion that attended some of my farewells. When I felt that troubling void of human connection as I traveled by boat from Malta to France, I was left with a heightened appreciation for everyone who came and went in my life—an appreciation I did not forget. All who lent their human warmth to my first year in London, offering their particular liveliness and meaning, became significant to me.

And so, after thanking the many people I befriended (while feeling a gratitude I alone was fully aware of), I gathered my bags and boarded a train that took me to Portsmouth, a port town in the southern part of England. Somewhere along the way, I learned that Portsmouth was the place where hundreds of thousands of Allied troops assembled for D-Day and Operation Overlord. This was the famous amphibious Allied invasion of France that finally freed Europe from Nazi Germany's cruel grip. But when my train arrived in Portsmouth, there was of course no sign of the many thousands of soldiers critical to the Axis defeat, just four years before. During those few intervening years, new life appeared and was now flourishing. For the first time in a decade, the war and everything surrounding it seemed strangely distant—present only as an atomized mist of memories belonging to those who survived.

The war's slow receding, its moving from the forefront to the background of our lives, was most noticeable to me, personally, once I discovered that, on the ship sailing from England to British Guiana, my fellow passengers were a small but convivial group. Their *joie de vivre* lifted me out of an underlying despair stemming from my long displacement, one I was unable to brush away. Some of these passengers were sailing to British Guiana for employment in Her Royal Majesty's Colonial Service, as I was. Quite a few were physicians. And one was that rarity in the post-war 1940s, a woman doctor. Our shipboard evenings were wonderfully lighthearted, with uproarious dinners full of humorous stories and much laughter. I behaved the way I might have, had my life not been derailed before the war. Later on, it gratified me that our enjoyment of one another's company did not end when we reached South America: some of these friendships lasted for many years.

Warmed, then, by the sun of jovial evenings aboard the steamer, my lingering feeling of loneliness, edged by a despair I tried not to feel, gradually vanished. It seemed as if a new stage of my life was beginning—one in which the earlier, war-induced difficulty and uncertainty dissolved at last. Though perhaps it simply disappeared beneath the surface of all those seas I sailed across, to arrive at the place where I found myself, now.

Our relatively small steamer sailed in a southwesterly direction after leaving southern England. Then we crossed the North Atlantic Ocean, heading for the immense continent of South America. There it would dock at Georgetown, the capital of British Guiana. On our fifth day at sea, I plainly saw the flat coast of our destination in the distance, with several church steeples rising like tall branchless trees against the blue sky. A few hours later, we landed and I disembarked, passing through the immigration formalities without incident. A staff member from the Public Hospital of Georgetown gave me a ride to a quite good hotel located in the center of the city. Later that day, I explored the surrounding streets and, in the evening, enjoyed a novel dinner of thoroughly curried rice seasoned with a bit of meat, in a pleasant restaurant filled with the scent of Indo-Asian spices.

The next morning I eagerly presented myself at the office of the hospital's medical director, a middle-aged man with a well-groomed beard, who proved both friendly and helpful. While Mr. Sheffield gave me a tour of the hospital's many interconnected buildings, he outlined its long history and described the institution's central importance to the community it served. Located on the eastern edge of the city, the Public Hospital occupied two large areas of land separated by a busy road. Toward dusk on that same day I carried my bags to the north side of this dividing road, and moved into a small apartment in a building where many of the hospital's physicians resided with their families.

Concluding our tour, Mr. Sheffield escorted me to a large medical ward reserved for patients who did not require surgery. He then announced that all eighty non-surgical patients were now my particular responsibility. During the ensuing week or so, I needed to fully examine each one, making sure the prescribed treatment was correct for each patient's condition, and that their written documentation was in order. My other responsibilities involved being in attendance when specialist physicians came to see particular patients on my ward, in addition to participating in weekly staff meetings for all those with supervisory patient responsibility. Though these duties represented a full day's work, every aspect carried its own appeal—from bedside visits with patients, to work in the diagnostic laboratory, to talking with specialists about the history of a patient's condition. All of it seemed novel and exciting to me in this new setting. Even the staff meetings were worthwhile, as they acquainted me with the mild-mannered politics of the place.

As months passed and I became used to my patient care duties and routines, I noticed that many patients were suffering from an illness I'd never seen before. "Tropical eosinophilia" was a disease characterized by fever, malaise, and persistent coughing, principally caused by an infiltration of microscopic parasites known as "filarial." However troublesome these tiny bugs were to my patients, they eventually proved quite beneficial to me: filaria stimulated my medical curiosity, and my first published paper was concerned with the effect of these parasites on human lungs. That paper, "Pulmonary Changes in Tropical Eosinophilia," appeared in the *British Journal of Radiology* some years after I first encountered this illness in British Guiana.

While my medical curiosity was finding new direction and focus, my social life at the Public Hospital was becoming more engaging. A small restaurant in one of the hospital's buildings was a gathering place for physicians and medical staff, and among the latter were quite a few attractive nurses. As a young unmarried physician, my popularity with these nurses was gratifyingly high, as I was considered a good prospective husband (though I was in no hurry to get married). Even so, I easily found a number of women eager for me to escort them to parties and dinners, those cheerful functions that defined our hospital social life.

In this way, time passed productively and happily, and my initial two-year tour of duty in Her Royal Majesty's Colonial Service came to an end. Preparing to return to London for a period of leave, I packed my bags once more and said my farewells (this time, with no unexpected welling-up of emotion), and after boarding an airplane for the second time in my life, I landed in Heathrow Airport many hours later.

As I tiredly walked off the plane and collected my luggage, my sole aim was to fortify my knowledge of tropical diseases, by undertaking a course of formal study. Finding a temporary hotel room not far from the University of London, I visited the British Colonial Office the next day. During a cordial meeting with an administrator whose pipe smoke lingered aromatically in the air around him, I requested a more permanent position. This he granted without hesitation, and we agreed that, after my six-month period of leave in London, I was to begin a three-year appointment in British Guiana. We shook hands and I left the Colonial Office to take a double-decker bus to the Ross Institute for Tropical Diseases.

Sitting at a small desk in the Institute, I filled-out all the enrollment forms for a program leading to the Diploma in Tropical Medicine and Hygiene, awarded by the University of London. Beginning my studies the next week, I soon learned that many clinical questions I had while attending my patients in British Guiana could be answered by studies archived at the Institute. I'm sure this realization nourished my interest in conducting my own research, and also encouraged my desire to contribute to the area of medicine in which I ultimately came to specialize.

But first, a momentous change in the circumstances of my life was about to occur. One morning, as I entered the Institute's long polished hallway, while quite conscious of being late for a class, I noticed a note with my name on it stuck to a message board. Removing this piece of paper, I read it hastily while rushing to my classroom. An administrative manager asked if I would kindly talk with a young lady about British Guiana, and life at the Public Hospital in Georgetown—for she was about to begin a term of colonial service as the hospital dietitian there. Our meeting took place the next day, in a conference room at the Institute. The "young lady," whose name was Betty Nield, was indeed young—just twenty-three years old—and quite pretty. In fact, I felt immediately drawn to her and thoroughly enjoyed our brief meeting, as she was an immensely likeable sort of person. But after answering her half-dozen questions within minutes, I was forced to disguise my disappointment that our conversation was ending so quickly. I shook her hand, wished her much success, and following a wordless pause, we went our separate ways.

Just three days later, as I was stepping off a bus outside the Ross Institute, there she was again, standing on a curb while waiting for the traffic light to change. Emboldened by my interest in her, I walked over and engaged Betty Nield in conversation, finally asking if I might join her for coffee. She agreed in the most polite way, and we set off to find a coffee shop where we might have breakfast together. This time, we spent several hours talking, both sensing that something special was evolving between us, as indeed it was. For we arranged to see each other every day after that, whether for breakfast or dinner. Our romance budded and soon bloomed, growing stronger by the day. Within weeks, we found ourselves in the euphoric state of being in love—unable to stop smiling in each other's company. It was all quite delightful and exciting.

Several weeks after the start of our serious romance, Betty told me that she was going home to Preston in north London to see her family for a few days. By then, we were thinking of getting married, and I asked if I might follow her there, provided her parents would allow it, with the specific purpose of discussing our marriage plans with them. Betty phoned some hours later to tell me I was indeed welcome in her parents' home, and I left by train for Preston straightaway. When I arrived and she opened the front door, we immediately fell into each other's arms, unable to restrain ourselves from kissing again and again. A few minutes later, we managed to compose ourselves, and Betty introduced me to her parents.

Her mother, Lillian, was tall and thin, a little nervous, but also quite warm and personable, like her eldest daughter. Betty's father, Edward, was on the stout side, red-faced and somewhat addicted to having his lunchtime beer at a pub each day, but also most pleasant. He owned a successful antiques business in the center of Preston, a store crammed with all sorts of furniture and porcelain, as well as glassware and paintings—all of which made a fascinating assemblage of museum-quality objects. In the world of antiques, the Nield store was quite well known, being one of the few outside London regularly invited for a famous exhibition in central London, each year, at the Dorchester.

Over the next several days, my relationship with both Betty's parents developed favorably, and I felt comfortable broaching the subject of marriage. They wholeheartedly approved, realizing that Betty and I were not only very fond of each other, we seemed unusually compatible. The

An informal photograph taken in London in 1948 around the time of my marriage to Betty Nield. I was then thirty-three years old.

marriage would take place at the Registry Office near the University of London because time was short, with our departure for British Guiana imminent.

The whole family attended our civil ceremony, including Betty's grandmother, her eighteen-year-old brother, Eddie (who worked in the family antiques business), and Eunice, her seventeen-year-old sister. I arranged for a fellow physician to serve as best man, and Betty and I both wore light-colored suits. After signing the marriage license paperwork, we exchanged our rings, and then off we all went to a celebratory dinner in a good London restaurant. Later on that evening, Betty and I discovered we each felt the heady, post-marriage-ceremony excitement of thinking we just became the luckiest person alive.

Since it was then near Christmas, we decided to spend our honeymoon in Austria's Tyrolean Alps in the town of Kitzbuehl, one of my favorite skiing resorts. During our ten days in my homeland, I reveled in the physical thrill of skiing deeply snowy slopes once more, among mountains that were both breathtakingly grand and gratifyingly familiar to me.

Betty was a good sport about attending a skiing school for beginners, telling me she would soon "catch up" so we might ski the same slopes. But we mostly enjoyed each other's company in the evenings, when we traded stories about our separate skiing adventures. I applauded Betty's progress in managing the "snowplow" technique that her skiing instructor spent several days teaching her class. But I couldn't help noticing that, everywhere we went, whether to the slopes, a restaurant, or simply walking around the lovely snow-covered streets, everyone was drawn to Betty the way I first was. She attracted admirers like a magnet: both men and women responded to her genuinely friendly, personable manner. Of course, this pleased me as the proud husband, however new and strange the experience of being married was—to both of us.

Toward the end of our stay, we took a train to my hometown city of Graz, so I might show my new wife some of the places important in my childhood. I felt as if I were seeing this familiar city for the first time through Betty's eyes: it all seemed absolutely novel, somehow, and a bit exalted. She even loved trying Austrian food. "So differently prepared," she explained, "from English fare."

In Kitzbuehl, we sampled *Tiroler Knödel,* or dumplings with ham, and also *Grösti,* a hearty combination of pan-fried onions, meat and potatoes. And *Schlipfkrapfen,* as well, a dish of ravioli-like pockets of pasta filled with potatoes and sometimes meat. For dessert, we shared *Apfelstrudel,* traditional apple strudel coffeecake, and *Kaiserschmarr'n,* a chopped pancake sprinkled with confectioner's sugar and fruit compote. Often, we ended our idyllic day by watching the setting sun as it turned the snow-blanketed Alps a brilliant pinkish hue. Standing on our hotel balcony a little later in the evening, we gazed at the stars: they seemed especially brilliant in the crisp winter air. And we toasted each other with small glasses of the locally brewed fruit schnapps.

Our fortuitous meeting at the Ross Institute, and the incredible coincidence that we were both going to work at the Public Hospital in

Georgetown, seemed to me another of those magical events that appeared in my life at just the right time. Each one helped me around yet another impasse, for which I could only be grateful—while wondering at life's unfathomable mysteries, all the more.

After less than two weeks, our all-too-brief honeymoon came to an end, and we reluctantly returned to London. During the next few days, we packed everything we mutually owned into several steamer trunks, in preparation for the boat trip from Southampton to British Guiana. I remember thinking that my luggage finally expanded beyond the two leather suitcases I carried since my exile from Graz. This seemed both momentous and natural, though I did not mention it to Betty. Instead, I quietly acknowledged this heartening change to myself, somewhat as if I wrote it down in some inner chronicle no one would ever see. But once we boarded our boat to British Guiana, our steamer trunks were stored God knows where, and we joked about hoping to see them again when we got to South America.

Many sea-days later, we stopped briefly at a series of islands in the West Indies—St. Kitts, French Guadeloupe, and Grenada. The climate on all three was so tropical, especially in contrast with Austria and England, that it seemed a little disorienting at first. But we soon slipped into the relaxing Caribbean warmth, claiming this time as an unexpected extension of our honeymoon. I found lovely tropical flowers for Betty, some of which she placed in her hair, which was then quite long. She, for her part, delighted in finding local dishes for me to try, many featuring coconut and West Indian spices. Overall, we spent a great deal of private time together, as behooves newly married couples, but at dinner we enjoyed the company of our fellow passengers. One passenger, in particular, I can still recall clearly. Louie Psaila was the son of a man who owned a very successful store in Georgetown, and Louie, Betty, and I enjoyed telling stories and being young together in a carefree way. During all the years that Betty and I lived in British Guiana he remained a good friend.

After our leisurely, two-week journey across the North Atlantic, we finally landed in Georgetown, where we managed to get all our steamer trunks and hand luggage stuffed into a single taxi which ferried us to the center of town. We rented a hotel room, and spent the rest of the day walking around the city, so I might introduce Betty to our new home.

Early the next morning, we both met with Mr. Sheffield, the Public Hospital's medical director, to discuss our new postings. Betty's job seemed formidable to me, as she was assigned supervisory responsibility for the dietary needs of well over four hundred patients, and would only be assisted in this task by kitchen and ward supervisors. For my part, I was given responsibility for two large patient wards, including the supervision of four junior physicians. And I was required to provide specialized advice, when needed, in all other parts of the hospital, including the outpatient department.

As with her Austrian ski school, Betty was once again a good sport. She quickly learned her way around the complicated hospital layout and became fully versed in the requirements of her job. But as both our positions were rather demanding and strenuous, we got into the habit of going to bed fairly early each evening, soon after dinner. In a month or so, though, after Betty came to know all my old friends, and we both made new friends, our social life became more active. The time we spent sleeping was greatly diminished, as a result, though we managed to keep this pace up without too many ill effects, since we were both so young and physically fit.

Later on, we purchased a small car and took weekend trips along the banks of the Demerara River which bordered the northern edge of Georgetown, before it flowed into the Atlantic. Our trips were punctuated by stops at local beaches, where we wandered the shoreline sand and went swimming. We also took more ambitious trips, journeying on some weekends farther into the country. On one occasion, we visited British Guiana's famous waterfall, the Kaiteur, and our photograph was taken as we stood on a rock jutting over the great cataract.

Betty and me in 1949, standing above British Guiana's Kaiteur Falls, one of the largest waterfalls in the world. The noise was deafening and the precipitous, 822-foot drop (over four times the height of Niagara Falls), made us almost dizzy with fear.

We played tennis, too, and even golf (a sport I pursued throughout my life, enjoying the challenge of it, along with the opportunity to be outdoors among rolling green hills). Betty, meanwhile, became accustomed to visiting the large produce market beside the river to purchase the ingredients for our meals—though our cook did most of the cooking, since both of us were working fulltime.

Then our life changed once more. Betty became pregnant. A very reliable Chinese obstetrician on the Public Hospital's staff took good care of her during the months her pregnancy progressed. And when delivery was near, she occupied a room in the Lady Thompson Ward—a restricted area on the hospital's top floor, both nicely designed and facing the ocean. In the early hours of September 14, 1952, our first son was born. We named him John, and were as happy as we could ever be. As a new mother, Betty seemed to glow from inside, as if our son had switched on a light before leaving her body. As a new father, I felt many things all at once: deeply moved, proud, and protective. It was quite extraordinary, the most all-encompassing experience I ever had, apart from falling in love with my wife.

To give ourselves a brief respite, while adjusting to our respective roles as parents in our brand new family of three, we decided to take a two-week holiday on the island of Tobago. Once attached to the South American mainland, this island sits above its parent continent like a child on a father's shoulders. We rented a small cottage and spent every day resting on the

Our first son, John, whom I loved dearly, giggling with me in the
porch hammock of our house in Georgetown, British Guiana.
This picture was taken many months after returning from our
two-week vacation in Tobago, following his birth. Betty and I
discovered that parenthood was a real joy for both of us.

beach, being careful to keep John out of the bright sun. We were becoming accustomed to a schedule of 'round-the-clock sleeping and feeding that governs the first months of a baby's life. And I was forever glad that we had this time to be together in uninterrupted peacefulness and solitude, while enjoying a lovely tropical paradise like Tobago. Soon enough, though, we returned to Georgetown to resume our jobs, and Betty had to leave John in the care of a nanny during the day.

Throughout this time, my medical practice was shifting away from its initial posting, and I was now caring for the population along the east bank of the Demerara River, as far as the airport and upriver from the city. In order to serve my east bank patients, I drove the road beside the river twice a day, stopping wherever there was a white flag at the roadside to indicate someone inside required medical care. Payment for my services was made on the spot, an arrangement that proved surprisingly lucrative. I also conducted an evening practice in the southern suburbs, using an office on the ground floor of a small house belonging to the district nurse. I visited the main hospital, too, usually once or twice a week. In addition to these several medical postings, I began to see patients in the ground floor office of our own house (by then, Betty and I were living in a cozy home with both a forecourt and a backyard garden, and even a garage for our car).

Betty with our son, John, in front of the sugarcane fields in back of our house in British Guiana. She devoted herself to taking care of both our sons and was an excellent mother.

Meanwhile, Betty was traveling into Georgetown proper to work half days as a nutritionist at the hospital. Eventually, she stopped working to devote her time to raising our little son, John. I can still remember how she looked after him so beautifully, delighting in the things he learned each day. She enjoyed reading to him and, when he was old enough to toddle along for some distance, took him for walks in the neighborhood.

I also spent as much time as I could with John, for I loved him dearly. As he got older, it became clear that he was a bright little fellow, keen to start learning some letters of the alphabet. He wrote them out carefully with crayons, and also worked out a few small problems with numbers. As a pediatrician, it pleased me to see that our son was a healthy boy growing normally, possessing a good appetite, tolerating his required immunizations well, and playing sensibly. We found a few friends for him in the vicinity, and they either played at our home, or his playmates' houses. From time to time, I wondered which member of our combined families John resembled. When he was little, such similarities were not clear, but in time it seemed he took after both Betty and myself. These things interest parents, and it occurred to me that my own parents may have wondered who my brother and I resembled, too.

All in all, this certainly seemed one of the busiest times of my life, with what amounted to four medical practices. But despite that schedule, Betty and I arranged to have something of a social life, accepting dinner invitations and giving dinners at our home. There was one aspect of my professional life, however, that eventually grew until it erupted—thus giving rise to the next episode of my career, and of my family's life as well.

My evening practice grew quickly, by word of mouth, until I was seeing an enormous number of patients each week. Their medical problems were not serious, only the usual minor illnesses, interspersed with common tropical diseases like malaria, dysentery, and, occasionally, eosinophilia. In time, I was seeing between fifty and sixty patients in the evening, each week, and only later realized that this influx was because my evening practice was now preferred over that of another physician's in the area. This physician, a Dr. Bissessar, had long enjoyed a thriving practice and was quite unhappy that his patients were defecting in droves. But since he was also a local politician, Dr. Bissessar was in a good position to craft a politically engineered solution. Realizing that the resident government radiologist was about to retire, he saw to it that I was selected to replace him. Of course, this meant I would need to return to London for a post-graduate diploma in radiology. In my absence, Dr. Bissessar hoped to regain his thriving practice, and once I returned, it would be as a radiologist who posed no further competitive threat.

This turn of events did not upset me at all. In fact, I was relieved. Though lucrative, my many medical duties were not only too taxing (I could not continue to work this hard much longer), but they were repetitive, as well, never engaging my medical curiosity—the investigative aspect of medicine that I so much enjoyed. But beyond these considerations, Dr. Bissessar's political maneuvering seemed to be yet another of those magical occurrences I was blessed with. For without his intervention, I might not have entered the field of specialization in which I later did my best work, making a contribution I was immensely glad to make.

So Betty and I packed all our belongings, putting some things in storage in our attic. We rented our house to a resident physician, hired someone to take care of our garden and car, and flew back to London. Since Betty's family had yet to see our son, John, we drove to Preston the next day and stayed with the Nields for a few weeks. Both Betty's parents were delighted with their first grandchild, and doted on him the whole time we were there, obviously loving him as we did. In the interim, I found a suitable apartment for our family, in a residential area not too far from the Manchester Royal Infirmary. Here I would complete my residency in radiology and earn my diploma in Medical Radiodiagnosis from the University of London. For the better part of two years, we lived in this apartment. John began kindergarten and made English friends. We socialized sporadically, and took trips into the countryside as a family, but Betty found this period difficult. There was so little that engaged her interest, and her days were a series of routine tasks at home, while waiting to take care of John when he wasn't in kindergarten. Going back to work as a hospital dietitian didn't seem like a good idea, so Betty was left with a lot of empty time and few social opportunities. She was forced to spend a great deal of time alone, and for someone as outgoing and friendly as she was, this was a great hardship.

But it was then the mid-1950s, and women everywhere were feeling stifled by society's expectations, yet unable to speak about what they felt. They couldn't bring themselves to acknowledge their unhappiness, even to themselves. The difficulty was largely with the idea that being a wife and mother *should* be totally fulfilling for women—despite the social isolation at home, and the absence of adult company during the day. I was not sure how to help Betty, nor was I even sure she wanted my help. We talked about various options, but nothing much came of it. In the end, time passed, and we made plans to return to British Guiana. Once we returned, I hoped our former friends would engage Betty, and that she would cultivate new interests.

The next three years in Georgetown passed quickly. They were full of interesting work for me, including published research, and new motherhood again for Betty. Our second son, Charles, had been born on November 5, 1955, just before we left London. We also rekindled our earlier friendships, and the malaise that afflicted Betty in London seemed to dissipate in the warm equatorial climate. Having two young boys to look after gave her plenty of distraction. And there were other young wives with whom she could go to the beach, taking the children along to play in the sand and swim in the ocean. Our family life appeared to find its balance again.

During this time, we also purchased a motorboat with an enclosed cabin, and spent many happy weekends exploring the Cuyuni and Mazaruni

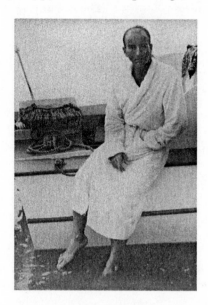

Here I am sitting on our boat, the "Draga," which means expensive or dear in Hungarian, during one of our many family trips. We often spent weekends navigating the rivers west of our home in Georgetown, British Guiana.

Rivers to the west of Georgetown. The boys loved these weekend adventures. We slept on the boat, went swimming, watched monkeys, and entertained ourselves with the idea of tigers stalking soundlessly through the jungle (though we never actually encountered even one).

It was during this time, as well, that I grew increasingly engaged in research and writing, and was excited by the possibilities of radiology. In one instance, I followed a patient's conjoined twins radiologically, prior to their birth, and wrote to a physician in London whose extensive research on the subject of such twins I'd read with interest. Our Georgetown twins were scheduled for surgical separation at the Public Hospital, and I invited this physician, a Dr. Thomas Smith, to visit me in British Guiana for the operation. My thought was that it would assist him in his research, since conjoined twins who are not stillborn were, and are, relatively uncommon (one in every 200,000 births). Dr. Smith cordially accepted my invitation, and was present for the surgery. But as often happens in these cases, only one of the twins was found viable and could be saved.

Afterwards, in the hospital coffee shop, Dr. Smith asked me something that, at the time, I found surprising. "What are you doing out here in the middle of nowhere? Why aren't you," he asked, "at the center of medical research back in London? Your skills are going to waste in a place like Georgetown."

I thanked him for his kindness, but was taken aback. In a few days, though, after I'd had time to think carefully about his comment, I began to see his point, and even felt he might be right. Betty and I talked about returning to London, so I might work in my field in a more active way, doing research and, I hoped, making a contribution to medicine. Our sons were growing quickly, and it seemed a good time to enroll them in a thoroughly English school, one with high academic standards. They were both bright boys. We loved the way of life in Georgetown, the ease of its tropical climate. But we knew that opportunities were limited for me, here, and in the end we decided to leave once more. I inquired about positions in London, wanting to have a job waiting for me before our return.

It would be some years before I realized that Dr. Smith's unexpected comment about my skills "going to waste" was itself another of those life-altering, magical occurrences that guided my life at intervals. It was a pivotal moment, a turning point necessary for what was to come next in my life and medical career.

CHAPTER SEVEN

London, England
Spring, 1960 ~ Fall, 1978

I n the spring of 1960, when my family and I left British Guiana for
the last time, our airplane landed first in the United States to refuel,
before it crossed the Atlantic Ocean and touched down, many hours
later, at Heathrow Airport in London. During our prolonged, two-
part flight, John and Charles, who were then eight and five years old,
slept in their seats beside Betty and me, or else entertained themselves
with card games and crayons. From time to time, they talked excitedly
about the clouds billowing mountainously outside our airplane's
windows. They also seemed enthralled by the glittering ocean so far
below, stretching endlessly in every direction. Later on, they exclaimed
over their first glimpses of land, as we flew over the eastern coast of the
United States; later still, they nearly shouted (we *shushed* them in time)
when the coastline of England became visible.

In the month or so before our permanent return to London, we
sold our house, our car, and our boat, in addition to all our furniture
and household goods, disposing of nearly everything we owned. We
left British Guiana with only a few trunks and suitcases full of clothes,

books, and personal items, some souvenirs from our travels, and the boys' games and toys. It reminded me of the years in my twenties and thirties when all my worldly belongings were contained within two leather suitcases. But I was now forty-five years old, no longer quite so young, and no longer alone in the world. Still, this move was very like starting all over again—as I had so many times before, prior to, during, and after the war.

Perhaps it was these thoughts that led me to remember the climate of official sentiment that existed when the war first ended (a sentiment firmly against appointing any physician not born in England, and especially not any physician from Austria or Germany). This memory, in turn, led me to recall my relief and gratitude when I found employment in a British colony. But in the dozen or so intervening years, and certainly by 1960, official sentiment drifted away from this strict anti-foreigner policy, and I was able to obtain a position at Royal Northern Hospital in London as an "attachment" radiologist, filling-in for someone on leave of absence.

But there was another lingering prejudice I was then struggling with: England's medical establishment tended to look down upon anyone practicing medicine in the colonies. It was, in fact, because of this tendency to view colonial service as "second rate" that Dr. Smith suggested I was wasting my time in British Guiana. As a result, I knew that I was about to face more hurdles when I returned to England, but told myself they were hurdles I could do something about. I would address them with a response long practiced—an almost muscular degree of determination—directed, this time, toward proving myself duly deserving of a medical career in England.

In the months following our arrival, we settled into a charming home in Jordan's village near Beaconsfield, a small town somewhat west of London.

Jordan's was an old village founded by Quakers, so it lacked a traditional English pub. It was additionally distinguished by an odd prohibition against cars driving through the village proper. They were only permitted to drive around it. Our new house in this lovely and eccentric setting was an English-style cottage, pleasantly ensconced within the quiet atmosphere of village life.

John and Charles were soon off to Repton Prep School in Darbyshire, located in another village, this one named for the famous English poet, Milton. Later on, they attended separate boarding schools; Kingswood for John and Rugby for Charles. Both our sons generally did well at school, with John excelling in sports (especially diving, swimming, rugby, and tennis), while Charles excelled in his academic studies.

We were now a thoroughly English family. Betty and our sons as young boys, with Charles on her left and John on her right, both enrolled at Repton Prep School in Darbyshire.

John did take it upon himself to deal with the school bullies at Kingswood, an activity he was, in due time, reprimanded for. Quite a bit later, he explained that he couldn't tolerate boys who bullied other boys. He was mercilessly bullied himself at Repton as a younger boy, because he had a German name. Other than that and enjoying sports, John rather precociously made the acquaintance of several young ladies who attended a girls' boarding school, just down the road from Kingswood. While his older brother was carrying on with girls and sports, Charles continued to apply himself to his studies, later graduating at the top of his class.

During these years, our family was together mainly on holidays and vacations. We took trips to Austria for skiing (the boys, like my brother and me, learned to ski at an early age). We also traveled to the Dolomite mountain range in northern Italy for hiking and climbing, and visited Yugoslavia, as well, where we all went swimming in the clear, cold lakes.

Meanwhile, my own adjustment to working in England was quite positive. I was delighted to find that I loved my job at Royal Northern, a very large hospital with many highly interesting cases for a radiologist. I found myself totally occupied and very busy, but happily so, since I was able to pursue my own specialized investigations. On any given day, anything at all might happen and I was never for a moment bored. Then, quite fortuitously, when my time at Royal Northern ended, I obtained an attachment post at St. Mark's Hospital for another year. At the end of this year, I was hired as a consultant radiologist at St. James's University Hospital in Leeds on a more permanent basis. A year after that, I was also appointed Senior Clinical Lecturer in Radiology, and Board Member of the Faculty of Medicine at the University of Leeds Medical School. My medical career in England was now firmly launched.

Betty did not fare as well: John and Charles were away at school most of the time, and I was always working. I came home each evening completely exhausted, and went off to bed not long after dinner. The next morning, I was up before dawn and off to the hospital for another long day. Weekends were little better. Sometimes, I was called into the hospital, but often I'd try to fit in a morning or an afternoon of golf. Betty and I attended social events together, mainly parties and classical music concerts, but she felt isolated and alone much of the time. Betty didn't know how to occupy herself in our empty house, and was far too often lonely.

Betty at the start of a social event, martini in hand.

Largely because she inherited a susceptibility to the disease of alcoholism from her father, she began to find solace in drinking. This later afforded her some company, as well: she made friends with a neighbor whose husband was also working most of the time, and the two wives spent every day consuming bottle after bottle of Scotch, vodka, or gin.

I didn't know what to do. My work had completely taken over my life, and I loved it. I was doing useful and fascinating research. But my marriage was suffering greatly. Again and again, I tried to help Betty by taking her to alcohol rehabilitation centers. And, again and again, she refused to stop drinking after treatment. It was what she clung to at this stage of her life. The whole thing was most distressing and painful for us both.

In the middle of this constant discord and personal tragedy, I was commuting to Leeds because of my appointment at St. James' and only home on weekends. This made matters all the worse for Betty. It was also apparent that I couldn't continue to commute back and forth. Leaving on Sunday night or Monday morning, I drove one hundred and fifty miles from London to Leeds, and stayed all week in "Bed and Breakfast" establishments. I wanted a less strenuous weekly routine, as well as a real home near my work. After searching the area thoroughly, I found a wonderful house, and told Betty I wanted to move there. She would not hear of our moving. We argued about this move, sometimes loudly, for weeks and weeks.

Finally, I left it up to her to decide whether she wanted to come with me to Leeds or not. And, in the end, she did. But even after leaving her

An English family portrait: our son, John, now a teenager,
on the far left; our son, Charles, nearly a teen, standing between
his brother and mother; and finally me on the far right
(like our sons, Betty and I are somewhat older).

drinking buddy behind in Beaconsfield, Betty continued to consume alcohol every day. She also smoked constantly. We both smoked for years, but when I turned fifty I finally said goodbye to cigarettes, not liking the constant coughing and unpleasantness. The fact that smoking led to cancer was not widely known in the sixties, so Betty continued to smoke, completely oblivious to the hazards.

During these years of unresolved tension at home, I was professionally hard at work, teaching and working with patients, in addition to writing research papers for medical journals. Papers of mine were published in the *British Journal of Radiology*, in *Clinical Radiology*, in *Lancet*, in *Gut*, and *Radiography*. I felt deeply compelled to do this work, and produced a never-ending stream of carefully constructed medical language, to describe my meticulously substantiated findings. Without thinking about it, I suppose it provided a sort of haven from the powerlessness I felt with regard to things at home—how I couldn't find a way to help Betty. Much like my own parents, we now lived in far different worlds, as this excerpt from the introduction to one of my research papers may perhaps illustrate.

"In the rapidly expanding field of vascular radiology, the value of angiography in visceral ischaemia is still disputed and its practice confined to few centres. The very high incidence of visceral artery atheroma, the considerable difficulty in evaluating such narrowing, and the strong likelihood of a prodromal symptomatology prior to vascular catastrophies, emphasise the need to clarify the role of visceral angiography." I then went on to describe those instances when angiography was useful and relevant—unlike alcohol rehabilitation which, I remember thinking, had sadly not proved useful at all.

Perhaps my unresolved home life added some fuel to my appetite for medical work; I can't be certain. But I do know that I loved medical research, and wrote several chapters for books during this time, chapters on "Angiography of Crohn's Disease," and "Angiography of the Visceral Vessels in Vascular Diseases of the Alimentary Tract," and "Aortography and Peripheral Arteriography." I also did extensive research on diseases of the pancreas, although my research was not at all related to the pancreatic disease of diabetes, an ailment from which both my father and older son suffered.

During this same troubling but productive time, a not unexpected but emotionally difficult thing happened: my mother, Elserl, died. I felt terribly saddened. We were friends all my life. In the late 1960s, after years of living in Israel with my brother's family (Pauli, his wife Margo, and son Ben), Elserl moved into an apartment in the Windsor Hotel in Haifa. Some

My brother, Pauli, who spent the rest of his life in Israel after our
exile from Austria in 1938, with his wife, Margo, and son, Ben.

time afterwards, she became ill and was hospitalized. One night, not long after she was released from the hospital, she got up and began packing everything she owned, saying merely that she was leaving. The next morning, she died.

Perhaps Elserl's intuitive self-direction was something my family generally possessed yet took for granted—though it thoroughly shaped some of our lives. When my older son John, for instance, began to follow his own wisdom (against my wishes for him to go to university and commit to a profession), I admit that I was not particularly sanguine about it. Though I did this very thing with my own father, by declining to enter the field he'd chosen for me— the exceedingly boring practice of law—in favor of the infinitely fascinating and marvelous world of medicine. Looking back, I see that John was compelled to make a similar intuitive choice for himself. Because, when he was eighteen and did not pass the entrance exams for university study, he hid this fact from us and ran off to London. There he did odd jobs to make a living, and soon became affiliated with a major photographic firm where he worked for two decades, getting married along the way, and having two children. But before John settled down, he experimented—as did many young people in those days—with everything the transatlantic Hippie youth culture offered. This distressed both Betty and me at the time, as it would most parents. Although, here again, I must admit that I committed my own youthful indiscretions. While at university, as a member of my fraternal organization, Charitas, I drank far too much on many occasions.

But my younger son, Charles, discovered his own talents in life in a less roundabout way, by first going to university and then becoming an accountant. From there, he entered corporate finance and cultivated a successful career which later took him to Germany and the United States, before he again settled in London with his wife and their three children.

In the beginning of our sons' marriages, Betty did not approve of the women either married. No one could possibly be "good enough" for her sons. This mutual disappointment created an unspoken familial divide, though there were other reasons for a feeling of divisiveness at home. I grew friendly with a radiologist at St. James' Hospital, a woman with whom I discussed my research findings, who understood my obsession with medical research. Our admiration for one another, and the fact that we worked together every day, combined with the ongoing difficulty at home, moved me in the direction of an involvement with my colleague.

When Betty learned about my affair, she responded by drinking even more, and I responded by working all the more. We were totally at odds with one another, and it seemed we could do nothing except end our marriage. In the end, however, we did not divorce. We'd been married since we were quite young, produced two sons, traveled and lived on two continents, and been together nearly half a lifetime. We were each other's closest family member, and it was not easy to dissolve all that we shared. Nor did I truly want to. Against all reason, perhaps, we remained together.

Betty and I, in the middle of our marital difficulties, did not divorce; instead, we sold our house and moved to the United States.

While all this was occurring in my personal life, I was working on some of the newer edges of radiological research, and was engaged in, among other things, double contrast studies of the stomach. It was this work that brought Dr. Igor Laufer, a young radiologist from Canada, to observe my methodology in Leeds. He introduced himself to me somewhat earlier, at a medical conference in London, where we both presented papers. Laufer was originally from Czechoslovakia—a European like myself—and we hit it off. At some point, I happened to mention England's mandatory retirement age for medical professionals, and how I was fast approaching that age (which was sixty-five), even though I wasn't at all ready to retire. I wanted to continue indefinitely, as I loved my work. He listened sympathetically and we kept in touch after he returned to Canada.

That same year, in 1975, I had an unexpectedly affirming experience, given that I was anxiously contemplating the impending end of my career. The European Association of Radiologists presented me with the Roentgen Medal at their Third Congress in Edinburgh. Wilhelm Conrad Roentgen, for whom the medal was named, invented the X-Ray in 1895, and this was the seminal discovery that gave rise to the field of radiology. I returned from this meeting with a modicum of hope: if my work was recognized to such an extent, perhaps there was one more fortuitous circumstance that might help me through this final impasse. Not long after, just such an event did occur.

Out of the blue, the young Canadian radiologist, Igor Laufer, called to ask if I was interested in a visiting professorship. He was just named chairman of a department of gastrointestinal radiology in the States, one newly formed at the Hospital of the University of Pennsylvania in Philadelphia. I hesitated no more than two seconds and accepted immediately. Betty and I flew to Philadelphia—only our second time on American soil—and spent a year in what then seemed to us a novel and energetic culture. I felt able to make a good contribution to the start of this new department, and felt quite welcomed there in return. But when the year ended, I returned to Leeds to await the inevitable—while still hoping for some miracle, something that would remove the impasse of forced retirement from my life's path.

I did not wait long. Laufer called within a month or so, to offer a permanent appointment at Penn. Betty and I both felt this was a new start for us, and that it represented an invigorating change from England and our long life here. We easily sold our house in Leeds, disposed of everything we'd accumulated in the attic and basement, along with most of our other possessions, and flew off into the next phase of our lives. I was tremendously hopeful again, and truly grateful for the removal of an impediment that threatened to end my medical career.

Years later, John told me how upset he'd been that, before we left for America, we cleaned out the attic and threw away the toys he'd played with so happily as a child. I can understand his dismay; it must have seemed we no longer cared that once he was our little boy. How hard it often is to understand those we most want to understand. But, at the time, the only thought Betty and I had was that our grownup sons surely had no use for their old toys, and so off they went to the dump.

Had I been a little wiser back then, I might have reminded John that life does not exist without loss—whether inflicted deliberately by strangers, or by a moment's thoughtless haste on the part of those who love us. There is no end to life's losses. But neither is there an end to life's generosity, to what may surprise us by happening next.

CHAPTER EIGHT

Philadelphia, Pennsylvania
United States
Fall, 1978 ~ Spring, 2005

The line of London passengers waiting to board our trans-Atlantic flight to Philadelphia was interminably long. But as Betty and I inched forward in this river of people, it seemed to us that we were not flying to a foreign country, but traveling to a familiar one. Perhaps because just one year had passed since my encouraging experience as a visiting professor at Penn. Whatever the reason, we adapted quickly to our new country and, soon after our arrival, found an apartment just across the Schulykill River, not far from the University's campus. A few months later, we moved into a rented house in a nearby suburb, intending to live there a short time, while looking for a more permanent home. But we eventually spent a full year house-hunting before finding the one we really wanted. Both of us were taken with this house— perched on a hilltop in Penn Valley on the Main Line—for similar as well as separate reasons.

I was enchanted by the large swimming pool waiting just beyond the patio that opened off the den. Nearly every evening in late spring and summer, and during the still-warm weeks of early fall, I dove into our pool, swimming as many refreshing laps as I could. It was a wonderfully relaxing way to dissolve the intense mental focus and concentrated physical energy that my work at the hospital demanded.

Betty enjoyed the water, too, but she especially loved the land at the back of our home. Many flowering trees grew on the acres that stretched behind the pool, and this lent a country feeling to what was a thoroughly residential neighborhood. We spent time together landscaping, creating beds of roses and a circular rock garden. This garden soon overflowed with flowers and strawberry plants, and their sweet red berries delighted us each summer. We planted more trees on our property, too, among them a blue spruce that particularly pleased Betty.

The interior of our home was filled with furniture my wife inherited from her father's famous antique store. When Mr. Nield passed away a few years earlier, his son Eddie took over the business, and shipped crates of charming and solidly built furniture to us in Penn Valley. Among many other pieces, there were several pre-Victorian-era round tables, a highboy cabinet, and a number of comfortable chairs. Gracing the rooms of our home with the soft glow of well-polished wood, these antiques warmed Betty with memories of her father's store and her family home in Preston.

Once we were settled-in, Betty found volunteer work that engaged her, becoming active in the "Nearly New Shop," a second-hand store that benefited Penn's hospital. This thrift store in Ardmore, not far from our home, was run by a group of women known as "The Doctors' Wives." Betty became a major force in making the store successful, largely because of her good mind and the business acumen she inherited from her late father. But the other tendency he passed along continued to be a concern, although Betty always functioned quite well, despite the alcohol.

Our lives during this time were more pleasant than they'd been in a long time, and our former difficulties diminished and faded away. We'd both slipped over the edge of middle age, though we agreed that the previous decade hadn't aged either of us overly much: I suppose we simply mellowed.

But despite the settling-down that came with our arrival at life's midpoint (I was then sixty-four, and Betty fifty-three), my work life was quite strenuous, and this period of my career saw the development of my most important contributions to radiology. Soon after my permanent appointment at Penn, I developed and perfected the double contrast enteroclysis technique for detailed imaging of the small bowel. I probably owe much of my success in

Wearing my University of Pennsylvania lab coat and standing before a lighted reader for diagnostic images. Though I was nearly retirement age when I arrived, I not only made the most important contribution of my medical career at Penn, I gave lectures all over the world during my twenty-five years on the faculty here.

this endeavor to a penchant for perfectionism—a trait that only extended to medicine (and perhaps golf)—or those areas in which I worked for many decades to perfect my knowledge and skills. Because it seemed reasonable to me that a more elegant way to obtain images of this most difficult-to-photograph bodily organ must exist, I worked steadily toward its discovery. There were minor setbacks along the way, but my years in radiology had given me a feeling for the field's "terrain," for what could be done and how, and I was determined to not give up.

Ironically, ten years later, my ability to persist came full circle in a sphere where no amount of persistence on my part would have solved the problem I then faced. In 1988, I was awarded an honorary doctorate from my old medical school in Graz, the same school I was forced to leave when

*Karl Franzen's University in Graz, my old medical school in
Austria, awarded me an honorary doctorate in 1988, fifty years
after I was exiled by the Nazis. My grandson, Benjamin,
is standing next to me, and Herbert Knoll, my best friend from
my early college days, is standing in the background. Of all the
honors and awards I received throughout my career,
this one meant the most.*

the Nazis annexed Austria in 1938. Because I refused to relinquish my dream of becoming a doctor, life eventually granted what was originally withheld: the medical degree I nearly earned, before being forced into exile from my native country. More than any other formal recognition, this honorary degree helped mend the feeling of betrayal by my country that I felt so keenly during the war years.

In 1933, I entered medical school in Graz almost timidly, not sure whether I was suited for this field of study, but eager to find out. And so, to finally receive a degree from my original school, some fifty years later, was more personally significant—for a host of reasons—than those who granted it could ever know. My elder son, John, and his elder son, Benjamin, both attended the ceremony in Graz. To me, this meant that three generations of Herlingers were present for a kind of family restitution—following our forced exile from Austria, and all the years pock-marked by the displacements and losses of World War II. Although the history behind the personally momentous quality of this occasion was not something I shared with my son and grandson, preferring not to burden them, or myself, with my painful past.

In the decades before and after receiving this honor, I was invited to present medical papers all over the world, and I happily delivered them in the language of the country I was visiting, whether French or Italian, German or English. By standing before those many podiums to share my discoveries with the medical community in each country, I found that I formed a bridge between the United States and Europe. I'd lived in both worlds and could communicate comfortably with people on both sides of the Atlantic Ocean.

Without a doubt, the single most important benefit of the peripatetic life I was forced to lead as a young man was this: it made me into someone who could represent an international approach to medicine. I was invited by university hospitals, as well as radiology and medical societies, to speak in a handful of states in this country (Arizona, California, Hawaii, Michigan, Minnesota, New York, and Pennsylvania), and in many countries around the world. Rome and Ancona, Italy. Taormina, Sicily. Crete, Greece. Frankfurt, Stuttgart, Munich, Leipzig, Bielefeld, Neuss, Dusseldorf, and Aachen, Germany. Elsinor, Denmark. Vienna and Graz, Austria. Brussels, Belgium. Leeds, England. Beunos Aires, Argentina. Beijing and Shanghai, China. Tokyo and Hong Kong, Japan.

Other opportunities for pursuing an international course of medical research and education arose, as well. In the early 1980s, I arranged to conduct courses in gastroenterological radiology with colleagues at the University of Vienna. These were attended by both Penn and Viennese medical faculty, and they were held at the incomparably grand Hofburg Palace, the former imperial palace and seat of the Hapsburg Dynasty.

Visiting this magnificent royal residence reminded me of the history I'd learned as a schoolboy in Graz. This history, about the Austro-Hungarian empire under Kaiser Franz Joseph, I recalled as the story of an empire which included within its borders not only Bohemia,

Tschechoslovakia, and the Balkan almost to the edge of Greece, but a few areas that were now part of Northern Italy. When I was born during the first year of World War I, the Hapsburg Dynasty was headed for dissolution. At the end of that war, it did indeed crumble and disappear. But what remained of the Hapsburg wealth and power was this lovely palace, the symbol of a grandeur not likely to return. Changes worldwide may have ended the dynastic rule of Austria and Hungary, I remember thinking, but *people* worldwide did not appear to change. The same passions and pursuits remained, regardless of which "dynasty" was in power.

During my time at Penn, I also found that I could create a bridge between my present and former professional homes—between Philadelphia and England—by arranging courses held in Leeds. For many years, I served as chairman for the annual "Gastroenterology for Radiologists" course held at St. James's University Hospital. This course brought British and American radiologists together, so they might study clinical gastroenterology from the perspective of practicing radiology, a useful marriage of two medical specialties. I very much enjoyed combining my collegial associations to create something new and useful to the field. Looking back, I would have to say that my second career in the United States ultimately blossomed in my most productive decades, ones that bore fruit from the entire orchard of my life's experience.

Betty, too, had found a productive way to express some of her many talents; she increasingly dedicated her time to making the hospital thrift shop a success. Partially as a result of this happy turn of events, we were completely unprepared and stunned when, in 1982, a malignancy on her tongue was conclusively diagnosed by a specialist. Betty never quit smoking, nor did she stop drinking, and this combination of assaults on her immune system had, over the course of several decades, turned deadly. But we faced her cancer together, and I saw to it that she received the best possible treatment at Penn. Those colleagues who treated her were every bit as conscientious with her care as I would have been myself, and her cancer responded well to treatment. For nearly three years, it was in remission. But despite the clear warning of her disease, Betty refused to stop smoking cigarettes, and when the cancer came back, it spread quickly, metastasizing from her tongue to the lymph nodes in her neck. By the spring of 1986, she was in constant excruciating pain and forced to take an array of painkillers, none of which could completely block her agony. They could only dull its jagged edges.

On May 16th of 1986, I drove to work in Philadelphia, knowing that Betty did not want to live any longer. We talked about it for months, and she was fully aware that she would never improve—that nothing medicine had to offer could help her. The future was sealed: it would be a slow and ever more painful decline. My habit was to call Betty at home by mid-morning, just to check in and give her a little boost, as she lay in bed trying to focus her attention elsewhere. The severe pain made concentration extremely difficult, and reading was out of the question, with television little better, so her days and nights were truly hellish. Usually when I called, she picked up on the second or third ring. But on this morning, I let the phone ring twenty times before replacing the receiver. At that point, I did not hesitate. Throwing off my lab coat, I spoke briefly to my secretary, and jogged to my car with my briefcase tucked under one arm. When I pulled into the driveway at home, everything was peaceful. The cheerful sound of spring birdsong surrounded me as I quickly opened the back door. Taking the hall stairs two at a time, I hurried to the bedroom. Betty's eyes were closed. I took her pulse from long habit, though I knew it was pointless, and then I sat down in a chair next to her bed.

Loss is beyond logic. It does not respond to rational thought. I knew that this decision of hers was best: the future held only suffering. But I sat with Betty in the silence of that room, oblivious to the birds singing outside, for a very long time.

Later on, I called Charles and John to tell them their mother passed away. Charles was then living in New Jersey, and John was in England, preparing to move to Turkey for his job. In a few days, our sons flew to Philadelphia for the funeral at a crematorium. Afterwards, I buried her ashes beneath the blue spruce she planted on our property in Penn Valley. Many years later, John took his mother's ashes back to England and planted them beneath a flowering laurel bush on his property.

But as I sat with my wife in the silence of that room, on the day of her death, part of what I was feeling was that she was so young—barely sixty years old. My father, when he was murdered at Dachau, was even younger: just fifty-seven. I found the brevity of both their lives profoundly disturbing, and the shortened lifespans of two people so important to me left a gnawing feeling. I was unable to come to terms with the sadness of their deaths for a very long time.

*   *   *

For many years, I belonged to Rolling Green Golf Club in Springfield, a suburb of Philadelphia, where I played golf several times each week in a foursome with three other men—Al Minisci, Vince Mace, and Joe

Cientofanti. A year before my wife's death, Al Minisci passed away. I was introduced to his widow, Billie, a tall woman and excellent golfer, at the club's sixtieth anniversary party. Billie and I began to golf together, and eventually we grew close, vacationing in Barbados, going to concerts, and attending other social functions as a couple. We enjoyed beating each other

Billie Minisci and I lost our spouses and comforted each other in our mutual loss; our relationship lasted many years.

at Gin Rummy, drinking single malt Scotch, talking about the differences between British and American English, and discussing liberal progressive politics, about which we largely agreed. Since we both lost our spouse, we understood the sudden void the other felt, and managed to partially fill that emptiness by being together.

But there was not a great deal of free time in my life—something Betty had long been unhappy about, as I well knew—since I was working fulltime at the hospital, traveling around the world giving invited lectures, and writing medical papers, book chapters, and books. Among the latter were eight books, all completed during these years. *Clinical Radiology of the Liver* in two volumes. *Double Contrast Techniques in Gastrointestinal Radiology. Clinical Radiology of the Small Intestine. Gastrointestinal Radiology Reviews. Advances in Gastrointestinal Radiology* in two volumes. And *Textbook of Gastrointestinal Radiology*, for which I was subeditor of the small intestine section and author of eight chapters.

This period at Penn was not just professionally active in an intense way; my personal life was also intense, for it was interleaved with losses and transitions. Three years after Betty's early death, I learned that my brother's prostate cancer was advanced, and that there was little time left. Pauli's son, Ben, who lives in Arizona, was flying with his family to Israel to see his father, and he invited me to come along. I hesitated, because there was so much work that I was responsible for at the hospital, but I ultimately decided to accompany them to Israel.

Ben Herlinger, my brother Pauli's son, with his wife, Dorit, and their sons, Ron (in the foreground), and Nir; they live in Arizona.

When the group of us walked into Pauli's room, my brother's eyes remained shut. He had the masklike facial pallor of someone very near death, and we were told that he was drifting in and out of a coma for several days. Ben bent down close to his father's ear and said, "Hans is here."

Immediately, Pauli's eyes opened wide. As he found my face among the many other faces in the room, his expression was utterly transformed. The masklike immobility disappeared, and his face burst into a brilliant smile of joy. Everyone was stunned, including me. Pauli could barely talk, and he made a few small sounds, but I went over to him and placed my hand in his, murmuring something reassuring, a few words I can't remember. I later learned that Pauli didn't believe I would make the trip to Israel, so he was overjoyed that I cared enough to come.

Only a few hours later, my brother passed away. The thought crossed my mind that he would see Father and Elserl, now. But on the flight back to the States, I several times saw Pauli standing among clouds outside the plane's porthole window, smiling his brilliant smile. This cheered me, even as I also thought, *Surely, this can't be real.*

*   *   *

That same year, in 1989, when my department at Penn was then thirteen years old, the head of GI Radiology, my friend Igor Laufer, decided to create a "Bar Mitzvah" to celebrate our departmental coming of age. This seemed like good collegial fun, especially as it was going to be held at the Wharton Sinkler Estate in Wyndmoor, another Philadelphia suburb. The estate was a magnificent treasure, an English Manor House built in the 1920s and willed to Penn half a century later. The university had long used it as a meeting and conference center.

As Billie and I drove down the long entrance lane to Wharton Sinkler on the appointed evening, I noticed that no one else was arriving. The parking area was already full of cars and there were no other people emerging from them. Puzzled, I picked up my invitation and checked the time. We were arriving fifteen minutes early. What was going on? In the estate's main building, we were directed to a large room and we walked into it, still mystified by the fact that everyone arrived before we did. Then Igor came over, and everyone turned to face us. "Surprise! Surprise!" they called out. Igor explained that the party was not actually for the department, but for me: it was my "non-retirement" party. After taking this in, I relaxed and we had a grand time. Dinner was interrupted by several speeches about my contribution to the department, and after dinner there was a lot of lively dancing. When Billie and I drove away, we talked about how kind it was of Igor and many others in the department to plan this party, in recognition of the fact that I was still working at the age of seventy-four.

An informal portrait taken during my years at Penn.
It was one of many photographs in a gift album presented during a
"non-retirement" party held in my honor and planned by
the radiology department in 1989.

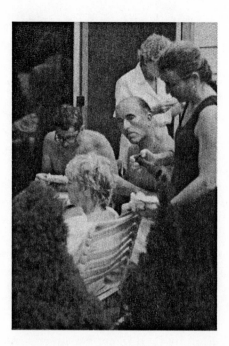

*Another photograph from this same album, showing me
(in the middle) at the annual radiology department pool party
that I held at my house in Penn Valley.*

* * *

Six years later, I was driving to Washington, D.C., accompanied by someone I'd known since my arrival at Penn as a visiting professor. When I first met Susan Bloom, she was a friendly radiology resident who often invited me to have dinner with her family. An excellent cook, she enjoyed hosting social meals. Susan and I later shared many impromptu dinners together at my home in Penn Valley, as well. No longer a resident, then, she was living in Reading, Pennsylvania with her husband, and stopped off to see me on her way home.

But Susan frequently urged me to visit the United States Holocaust Memorial Museum in Washington, D.C., an institution both of us made donations to, yet I did not relish the idea of going there alone. So, one spring morning, she and I drove down there together, talking as we usually did, about work and developments in both our lives. But after we arrived in Washington and entered the museum, our mood completely changed.

Along with a crowd of other visitors, we were stuffed into a claustrophobic metal elevator designed to resemble the boxcars that transported Jews to the concentration camps. We each clutched a passport belonging to someone who perished in the camps—a museum feature intended as our "passport" to imagining the Holocaust as happening to us personally, instead of to millions of easily distanced strangers.

In my case, that wasn't necessary. Soon after we crowded into the elevator, feelings about the Holocaust that I concealed in order to lead a productive life, stirred inside the tightly sealed box where I confined them. As they banged loudly against the walls of this inner container, I felt caught inside an enormous echo chamber—a sensation magnified by the fact that Hitler's booming and maniacal voice was now assaulting us everywhere we went. His voice seemed to reverberate within us as we walked from exhibit to exhibit, descending from one floor to the next by crossing to each new elevator on catwalks. I held on to Susan's hand tightly, feeling the terror my Hungarian relatives must have felt when the Nazis arrested them at the end of war (and as I was forced to assume because of the historical record, transported them to the death camps).

When we arrived on the final floor, I scanned each name on the wall, looking for the names of my relatives, but found not even one. Neither did I see any faces I recognized in the photographs displayed on the other floors, or recognize any shoes in the mountain of shoes taken from those who were gassed and cremated. And so, despite all reason, I began to hope that—since my relatives' names were nowhere to be found—perhaps they escaped at the last minute (unsuccessfully, I felt myself trying to not become too attached to this desperate idea). But on our drive back to Philadelphia, the grim emotional weight of what we saw that day made our usual conversation impossible. We drove the entire hundred and forty-five miles in absolute silence.

*   *   *

In 1996, the Society of Gastrointestinal Radiology awarded me the Cannon Medal for "outstanding contributions to Gastrointestinal Radiology"— meaning my work on the small bowel. This medal was considered the highest award in my field and I could not help but be greatly honored. The presentation ceremony was held in Bermuda, and fifty or so of my former radiology trainees, as well as members of my department at Penn, flew down to celebrate this recognition of my lifetime achievement. My sons and their families flew down, as well, and on the day of the official ceremony, there

*My elder son, John, with his wife, Jan, and their sons,
Benjamin (left) and Toby (right).*

*My younger son, Charles, with his wife, Diane, and their three children,
William (far right), James (middle), and Katie (far left),
on a skiing holiday.*

was a departmental party. My friend, Susan Bloom, happened to be talking with my older son, John, at this party. Their conversation turned to the subject of my parents and their ordeal during the war. For many years, John heard almost nothing about his paternal grandparents; neither did he hear very much about his father's childhood, or how I spent the war years. I did not want to harm my sons with painful stories about my ordeal. It seemed too distressing to talk about when they were children, and later on, there was never a good time to bring it up. My attention was not on the past, anyway, but on medicine. But there was a deeper reason, too. If they didn't know about my side of the family, they could avoid being Jewish— something I didn't want my sons to be—simply because I didn't want anybody I loved to go through what I had during the war.

Of course, both John and Charles were adults now. They quite naturally wanted all the pieces of our family's past brought together, so they would know the whole story of their heritage. Susan, meanwhile, urged me repeatedly to write a book about my life, as I sometimes thought about doing. But my time was so occupied by my work, I was only able to jot down a few pages of notes. Later on, of course, it seemed that life conspired to help me write my memoir. But before that happened, there was another difficult transition to undergo.

I was now eighty-three, and gradually I accepted that my house in Penn Valley was too much for me to take care of: the pool alone required a lot of seasonal care. With great reluctance, I sold this house that I loved so much. A friend told me about a pleasant retirement community called the Quadrangle, which was located in Haverford, about ten miles from Penn Valley. I found a small cottage there and, before I moved, shipped most of our family furniture to my sons in England, taking with me only what fit into my new home.

Once I settled into the Quadrangle, I made a marvelous discovery: if I left for work early enough, I could drive to the hospital without stopping for a single traffic light, as they were still switched off in the early hours of the morning. I was always a rather fast driver (some would call that an understatement), although I'm not sure why—except that certain things cause me to feel exceedingly impatient. I do not like to wait around and waste time. Early in my life, I was at the effect of outside circumstances so much, that I suppose I have little patience for things resembling that kind of confinement, now. In any case, not having to stop for traffic lights delighted me. I could get to my desk before seven in the morning, and work hard on my writing, whether articles or books. Then I could check in with colleagues, and perhaps do one or two consultations regarding their patients. And I could still leave in time for an afternoon round of golf at Rolling Green. This was a good way to live, it seemed to me, for someone in his eighties.

*I have always loved to play golf. On this course in Hawaii I am
emerging from the vicinity of a sand pit, with several white balls
visible in the background. Of course, I no longer remember
which golf ball was mine.*

Several weeks after I moved into my new cottage, I began meeting
other residents at the Quadrangle and making friends. Then, just before I
left for a brief trip to England and Austria, I met an interesting woman
named Betty Schmidt at a gathering of Quadrangle residents who played
Bridge on Monday nights. Betty and I spent a few evenings together, having
dinner and talking, and when I returned I gave her a souvenir from my
trip: a small Austrian vase. I noticed that she enjoyed flowers. Since Betty and
I lived in the same community, it was easy for us to spend time together, and I

*My friend, Betty Schmidt, and me, before a dinner party
in my cottage at the Quadrangle.*

soon became absorbed by the social life in this small community, enjoying the varied company so readily available there.

After she got to know me better, Betty began to insist—just as Susan Bloom, Billie Minisci, and other friends insisted earlier—that I think seriously about writing my memoir. I decided to make more notes, but knew that one part of my family's story remained an unanswered question in my mind, one I still needed to answer. Writing to the United States Holocaust Memorial Museum in Washington, I was put in touch with an archivist, Mr. Ferenc Katona. If I wanted to know the fate of my Hungarian relatives, he advised me that a meeting with members of the museum's staff might be helpful. I asked Betty to accompany me to Washington for that meeting, as it still seemed too hard to go there alone.

The staff members who met us in the museum's lobby were quite gracious, and after we took the elevator to the research area and placed our belongings in a locker, a librarian from their Survivors Registry Department escorted us to a long table and offered chairs. He then placed a stack of five or six large books with tissue-thin pages on the table in front of us. Together we looked through these books, a listing of survivors, alphabetically arranged. I was looking for the following names:

Jenö Bauer
Jenny Bauer
Lajos Szente
Clody Szente
Ignác Löwenstein
Paula Löwenstein
Pista Löwenstein
Zoltán Löwenstein
Gustav Friedrich
Aranka Friedrich
Edith Friedrich
János Biró
Lizzie Biró

Though we searched the thin pages of those large books for nearly an hour, we were unable to find even one name. As we closed the books, and the librarian began to gather them up for shelving, I could feel tears sliding uncontrollably down my cheeks. *They had not escaped.* I quickly brushed the tears away with the back of my hand, and the librarian said nothing, though he seemed upset on my behalf, as did Betty.

I thanked him for his efforts, trying to sound appreciative, though this confirmation was deeply painful. We then met with Ferenc Katona, the archivist with whom I corresponded some months ago, and he agreed to continue searching for the name of my favorite cousin, Zoltán Löwenstein. There was a chance, in Zoltán's case, that the outcome would be different.

But the next day, I received an email from Katona regarding my cousin's fate. I replied with these words:

"You have been more than kind to have given me an entire hour of your time, when I visited you yesterday. It has been a deeply felt day of sadness, a day that I had been putting off for years. The outcome was not unexpected. Nobody survived; all failed to return from wherever they had been taken. Thank you so much again for your email, and for the confirmation of Zoltán Löwenstein's non-return as well. There seems, therefore, to be no reason for me to write to Zalaegerszeg. However, I will be thankful to you should you let me know of any additional information you might get out of Zalaegerszeg, during your stay in Hungary. Zoltán was a very smart person, and I would not be surprised if he managed to survive somehow. He was also highly successful with women and very much needed their company. He may well have got married and there might just be an offspring somewhere.

Please do keep me informed of any further information that might concern me. Also please do let me know if you might come to Philadelphia at any future time, as I would value a further meeting with you so very much.

Again, my sincere gratitude for the kind reception you gave my friend and myself, and for the intense preparatory investigation you had carried out before we met."

Mr. Katona located Zoltán's name in a list of Jews who, on May 1, 1944, were living in Zalagereszeg, Hungary. There was a handwritten note on this list which explained that names marked with an "X" belonged to those people who returned. Beside Zoltán Löwenstein's name, there was no "X."

After completing more intensive research, Katona learned that Zoltán was married in the spring or summer of 1944 and subsequently drafted for a forced labor battalion. He and six others in his battalion of laborers were reportedly hit by a truck, in the early months of 1945, in a town north of Zalaegerszeg. This "accident" was most likely a deliberate murder. Zoltán's wife was then deported to a concentration camp. But she managed to survive, return to Hungary, and remarry. She then lived in the town of Keszthely as Mrs. Miksa Müller.

My other relatives perished, there could be little doubt, because the Jews of that region, in Zalaegerszeg, Körmend, and Szombathely, were all arrested and deported to Auschwitz in 1944. Children, the elderly, and the sick were murdered immediately upon their arrival, while those judged fit for slave labor were transferred to camps like Buchenwald and Bergen-Belsen. There they were killed with guns, malnutrition, exhaustion, or some combination of these. Very few survived, and fewer still escaped.

* * *

The year the World Trade Center was destroyed, in 2001, was the year that Betty Schmidt and I went to the United States Holocaust Memorial Museum to learn the fate of my relatives. It was also the year that Betty fell and fractured her leg. Surgeons implanted a long metal bar, hoping that the femur, her long leg bone, would knit together and become stable enough for her to stand. But they weren't sure whether she would ever walk again. I decided to surprise Betty with something that couldn't fail to take her mind off her troubles.

My beloved miniature dachshund, Jackie, had been dead for several weeks, her ashes interred in a small cedar box on which I'd placed a plaque that read, *Jackie, The Light of My Life*. This box was now enshrined on my dresser, and I missed her every day.

But when I happened to see an advertisement for dachshund puppies at a breeder sixty miles from Philadelphia, I knew that I must go see them.

After I got back, I put a box on Betty's bed. The lid was closed, but the box moved.

Betty looked at me, strangely, as if she perhaps thought I was slightly deranged.

"Are you nuts?" she, in fact, said. This question was not entirely asked in jest.

"Open it," I said, smiling my most mischievous smile.

So Betty did, and a tiny puppy scrambled up the side of the box, and licked her face.

She smiled. And the puppy smiled back.

"I'm going to go play golf," I announced.

"But, Hans . . ." Betty wailed.

"I'll be back later on."

The next day, we gave her a name, and Maggie proved very fastidious: wherever we spread newspapers on the floor to paper-train her, that was precisely where she would *not* go.

As I hoped, this gave both of us plenty of things to think about, aside from our own problems. Maggie was also very good at curling up in laps, chasing balls, riding in cars, and going for walks. As she grew bigger, maturing quickly from her puppy size of one and a half pounds, she trained us very well. We learned to stop putting down newspapers. As Maggie knew all along, they were far easier to read if they weren't scattered around on the floor.

Every night, Maggie finds a spot in the crook of my arm and promptly falls asleep, not moving until I get up before dawn (Jackie has long since laid claim to the crook of my other arm).

Maggie and me in our backyard at the Quadrangle.

*   *   *

Two years later, when I was eighty-eight, I decided it was time to formally retire from my emeritus position at Penn. The department held a luncheon in my honor, and I was showered with speeches, cards, presents, and kisses. They made a tremendous fuss over me, for which I was grateful.

The next day, when I got up in the morning, I remembered that I didn't have to go to work. There was an emptiness in that—a rather large emptiness. So I began to work on my memoir in earnest.

To my amazement, two years of official retirement passed quickly, and I filled those years with travel, golf, and work on my memoir. This book was nearing completion, with just two chapters to go, when Betty insisted on a birthday party to celebrate my ninetieth year—one that would include my extended family, all my friends and former girlfriends, my golf buddies, my Quadrangle friends, and my medical friends and colleagues. The prospect seemed a little overwhelming. But I agreed to it, because I wanted to bring everyone together.

A day or two before my ninetieth birthday on April 19, 2005,
celebrating this occasion with members of my family and friends.

Ninety people were invited, and most were able to come. A few of those in Europe sent beautiful letters with their regrets, but many did fly across the Atlantic for my birthday party. It was held in Narberth, not far from the Quadrangle, and after reception cocktails at the restaurant's bar, we assembled at round tables for dinner. Each table had a centerpiece featuring the flag of a country I lived in—before, during, and after the war: Austria, Italy, Malta, Palestine, Uganda, England, British Guiana, and the United States. Midway through dinner, my sons, John and Charles, stood to toast the occasion of my ninety years. Others stood, as well, to speak generously about our friendship.

During dinner, a few people wandered onto the dance floor in small clusters, but now nearly everyone was up and moving around the floor. There were line dances and circle dances, slow dances and fast dances. Even the youngest kids were having a good time. Betty was here and there, taking care of things, making sure everything got done.

At some point in the festivities, the microphone was passed around the dance floor so friends and family could take turns singing "Happy Birthday" to me in German and French, Israeli and Italian. I responded in their language of choice. Then Betty and I were hoisted in our chairs above everyone's head by four strong men, while everyone danced around us in a circle (I suppose this was my combination Bar Mitzvah celebration and ninetieth birthday party, and that the Rabbi of Graz was secretly pleased).

Later on, I began to think of all those who were not here to celebrate with us. My Hungarian aunts and uncles. Elserl and Father. Zoltán. Lizzie Biró. Pauli. My wife, Betty.

Though perhaps they *were* here—I just didn't know how to see them. As if in response to that thought, the face of Father Laspina appeared in my mind's eye.

It was then I remembered that fall day in Trieste. The day when I looked out to sea, wishing for a solution to my plight.

My wish was surely granted. From that day forward, a path always opened at my feet. It was the path I have followed all these years.